YOUR LIFE'S PURPOSE

in

GOD'S GRAND DESIGN

Your Life's Purpose in God's Grand Design

YOUR LIFE'S PURPOSE
in
GOD'S GRAND DESIGN

Richard Ferguson

Your Life's Purpose in God's Grand Design by Richard Ferguson
Copyright © 2023 by Richard Ferguson
All Rights Reserved.
ISBN: 978-1-59755-763-4

Published by: ADVANTAGE BOOKS™
Longwood, Florida, USA
www.advbookstore.com

This book and parts thereof may not be reproduced in any form, stored in a retrieval system or transmitted in any form by any means (electronic, mechanical, photocopy, recording or otherwise) without prior written permission of the author, except as provided by United States of America copyright law.

Unless otherwise indicated, Scripture quotations taken from The Holy Bible KING JAMES VERSION (KJV), public domain.

Scriptures marked (NKJV) are taken from the Holy Bible NEW KING JAMES VERSION®. Copyright© 1982 by Thomas Nelson, Inc. Used by permission. All rights reserved.

Library of Congress Catalog Number: 2023946531

Name: Ferguson, Richard, Author
Title: *Your Life's Purpose in God's Grand Design*
           Richard Ferguson
           Advantage Books, 2023
Identifiers: ISBN: Paperback: 978159757634,
               eBook: 9781597557733
Subjects: RELIGION: Christian Life – Inspirational

Evangeline Ferguson: Lead Contributor and Lead Editor

First Printing: October 2023
23 24 25 26 27 28   10 9 8 7 6 5 4 3 2 1

Your Life's Purpose in God's Grand Design

Dedication

To You Our Lord and Savior:

This book is a love letter to you my dear Heavenly Father, to our Lord and Savior Jesus Christ and to the Holy Spirit which proceeds from thee. We, your sacred children, give you thanks and praise and our deepest gratitude for all you have done in the creation of us your children.

Never in my life did I think that you dear Father would select me as your messenger and be a co-author in any book that I write. But you did as is shown within these pages. Your direct involvement in the words spoken herein have shined a bright divine light in magnificent detail about your creation and how it all fits together for the benefit of your sacred children. It is you dear Father that are the centerpiece for the thoughts written for your children on earth.

Thank you, dear Father, for describing in detail why you created the spiritual and physical realms to fit so tightly together matching your children's physical bodies. Out of nothingness, this creates a pathway for us to come back to you in the Heavenly Kingdom and heal from the ravages of Satan's rebellion and the sinfulness of Adam and Eve.

I must thank my Lord and Savior Jesus Christ. Remember always dear reader I am not the only author who wrote this book for it is our Lord and Savior Jesus Christ who co-wrote it from beginning to end. This is also with my ever so constantly loving Blessed Mother Mary. Both were always at my right shoulder the entire time day and night speaking silent loving sacred thoughts while this book came to fruition. Without Jesus Christ and Mother Mary this book could not have become what it is today.

In the name of Jesus Christ, Amen.
Richard Ferguson

Your Life's Purpose in God's Grand Design

Table of Contents

DEDICATION 5
INTRODUCTION 12
1: HOW THIS BOOK CAME TO BE 14
    A STORY OF DIVINE LOVE 14
    TWO BEAUTIFUL DIVINE SPIRITUAL FIGURES APPEAR TO ME 15
    MY PERSONAL COVENANT WITH ALMIGHTY GOD 16
    THE SUBJECT MATTER OF THIS BOOK 17
    MY DIVINE PURPOSE 19
    FOR CLARITY'S SAKE 20
    A NOTE FROM ALMIGHTY GOD: 20
    MY FATAL SICKNESS 21

2: THE HEAVENLY SPIRITUAL WORLD TODAY 24
3: A CHRONOLOGY OF EVENTS 25
4: OUR MAGNIFICENT STORY BEGINS 29
    SECRETS, THEY ARE IMPOSSIBLE 30
    THE TIME WE SPENT WITH GOD IN HEAVEN 31
    GOD'S CHILDREN MUST MAKE A CHOICE 32

5: THE HEAVENLY REALM 35
    THE HEAVENLY KINGDOM 35
    SOME DETAILED QUESTIONS ABOUT THE HEAVENLY KINGDOM 36
    ALMIGHTY GOD ANSWERS THE QUESTIONS ABOVE 37
    MORE QUESTIONS FOR ALMIGHTY GOD 42
    ANSWERS FROM OUR LORD JESUS CHRIST 43

6: THE CHARACTER OF ALMIGHTY GOD 48
    THE BIBLICAL LIST OF GOD'S ATTRIBUTES OR CHARACTER 48
    HOW TO TALK DIRECTLY TO OUR HEAVENLY FATHER 51
    ALMIGHTY GOD IS A VERY PERSONAL GOD 52
    AN UNEXPECTED LOVING ENCOUNTER WITH ALMIGHTY GOD 53
    HARD TO BELIEVE, BUT TRUE 55
    OUR BLESSED MOTHER MARY ALWAYS IS WATCHING OVER ME 55

7: WHAT EXISTED BEFORE CREATION 57

8: THE DECISION TO CREATE SACRED CHILDREN 61

CREATING GOD'S SACRED CHILDREN/ A PERSONAL DISCUSSION 61
THE COMING ETERNAL CHOICE FOR EACH OF US 64
THOSE WHO CHOOSE NOT TO GO TO EARTH 64
BEFORE WE ARE BORN TO EARTH 65
STORY OF ME SEEING MY FIRST GRANDCHILD BEFORE HER BIRTH 67
THE SHAPE OF BABIES STILL IN THE SPIRITUAL INCUBATOR IN THE KINGDOM 68
THE FUTURE 69

9: DESIGNING GOD'S SACRED CHILDREN 71

10: A POETIC VIEW FOR BOTH OF GOD'S CREATIONS 76

11: GOD CREATES HIS CHILDREN IN THE SPIRIT 79

12: THE VERY CORE OF GOD'S MAGNIFICENT SACRED CHILDREN 83

POTENTIAL SACRED CHILDREN SIN 84

13: THE MAGNIFICENCE OF GOD'S INTERLOCKING CREATIONS 88

GOD PROVIDES HIS SACRED CHILDREN THE OPPORTUNITY TO RETURN TO HIM IN HEAVEN 89
NOTHING BY CHANCE 90
EVOLUTIONISTS & ATHEISTS 90

14: THE DIMENSIONS AND STRUCTURE OF CREATION 93

TIME 93
DIMENSIONS 94

15: ALMIGHTY GOD CREATES THE SPIRITUAL REALMS 96

WHEN WAS THE SPIRITUAL REALM CREATED? 96
CREATING THE SPIRITUAL REALM 96
PERSONAL SPIRITUAL COMMUNICATIONS BETWEEN GOD AND HIS CHILDREN 98
THE SPIRITUAL REALM IS WHERE SATAN AFFECTS GOD'S CHILDREN 100
A SHORT HISTORY 101
WHY A CREATION OF THE SPIRITUAL AND PHYSICAL REALM TOGETHER? 103
OUR HEAVENLY FATHER EXISTS WITHIN AND THROUGHOUT ALL CREATION 104
THE SPIRITUAL AND PHYSICAL REALMS WORK TOGETHER 104
THE PARALLEL CHARACTER WE HAVE WITH JESUS 106
A REAL STORY WITH ME USING THE AKASHIC RECORDS 107

16: ALMIGHTY GOD CREATES THE PHYSICAL REALM 109

WHY GOD CREATED THIS PHYSICAL UNIVERSE 109
MANY DIFFERENT TYPES OF GOD'S CHILDREN 110
A WONDROUS MEETING PLACE FOR THE CHILDREN OF GOD 111
IRREDUCIBLE COMPLEXITY: 113

17: THE HOLY SPIRIT AND CREATION 120

18: ADVANCED SCIENCE PROVES GOD IS THE CREATOR 123
- These Scientific Discoveries Prove God Is The Creator 123
- The Two Major sections of science 125
- The Creation of the Physical Universe 126
- Scientific Parameters That Must Be To Support Life On Earth 127
- Our Magnificent Physical Universe 131
- Modern-Day Scientific Knowledge Tightly Links Creation And Science Together 132
- The Basis Of Scientific Investigation and Discovery: 134
- The Objective Scientific Data 134
- Evidence for the Fine Tuning of the Universe: 135
- A Few Examples Of Creation's Fine-Tuning 135
- Necessary galactic relationships For Life To Exist 136
- Factors That Determine The Probability For Attaining Life Support On Our Planet   137

19: GOD CREATES THE HUMAN BODY 139
- The Cellular Level 145
- Human Genome And Chromosomes 146

20: LUCIFER, THE THREAT AGAINST GOD'S SACRED CHILDREN 148
- Satan Thrown Out Of Heaven 148
- The Spiritual Realm Is Where Satan Affects God's Children 154

21: WHAT HAPPENED IN THE GARDEN OF EDEN 156
- Creation Is Specifically Designed For Redemption 156
- A Deep theological Question For A Child Of God 157
- The Garden of Eden 157
- A Very Special Place, The Garden of Eden 158
- Question: How Does The Imperfect Arise Out Of The Perfect 159

22: INESCAPABLE HELL 163
- How hell fits into God's creation 163
- Why Hell Still Exists 163
- God's Children and Hell 164
- Why Can Satan Still Enter Heaven? 164
- God Gives his Children Every Possible Opportunity To Enter Heaven 166

23: GOD PREPARES REDEMPTION 169
- The Role of Jesus Christ 169

24: WHO REALLY IS JESUS CHRIST IN OUR LIVES? 173

25: WHERE PERFECTION MEETS SIN 175

26: OUR BLESSED MOTHER MARY 177

- AN ANGEL APPEARS 177
- MARY SPEAKS ABOUT WHEN GOD'S ANGEL APPEARED TO HER 177
- ANGEL DEPARTS OUR BLESSED MOTHER MARY 180
- OUR BLESSED MOTHER MARY - THE BIRTH OF JESUS 182
- ON JESUS BECOMING HUMAN 185

27: JESUS TRAVELS WITH HIS GODLY MESSAGE 189

- HIS FAITHFUL COMPANIONS 190
- HIS MISSING YEARS, WHERE HE WENT AND WHAT HE DID 191

28: JESUS ARRIVES IN JERUSALEM AND THE CRUCIFIXION 194

29: THE CRUCIFIXION 200

30: FURTHER COMMENTARY 203

- THE CRUCIFIXION OF JESUS CHRIST 203
- 1950'S STYLE UNDERSTANDING REGARDING THE BLOOD OF JESUS 204
- WHY THE CRUCIFIXION HAD TO HAPPEN 204

31: THE ASCENSION OF JESUS CHRIST 207

- PERSONAL COMMENTARY FROM JESUS 208
- JESUS ASCENDS TO HEAVEN 211

32: PURGATORY 212

33: ENTER INTO THE HEAVENLY KINGDOM 213

- A POETIC VIEW 213

34: WHAT HAPPENS WHEN PEOPLE DIE? 215

- AFTER DEATH, EVERYONE ENTERS THE SPIRITUAL REALM 215
- A LIFE REVIEW IS CONDUCTED 216
- SOME ARE DESTINED FOR INESCAPABLE HELL 217

35: WHAT HAPPENS WHEN UNREPENTANT SINNERS DIE? 218

36: SPIRITUAL WARFARE 220

- THE COSMIC SPIRITUAL WARFARE SITUATION 220
- SPIRITUAL WARFARE AND THE FALL OF AMERICAN CHRISTIAN VALUES AND PRINCIPLES 221
- SPIRITUAL WARFARE AND SATAN'S AGENDA 222
- MY FIRST AND DIRECT PERSONAL ENCOUNTER WITH SATAN VERY SCARY! 224
- ACTIONS 225
- HOW TO DEFEAT SATAN IN A WORLD OF SPIRITUAL WARFARE. 226
- THE BEST WAYS FOR CHRISTIANS TO WIN THE SPIRITUAL WAR 227

37: WHAT HAPPENS WHEN WE PRAY? 229
Almighty God hears every prayer 229
It will be granted if it's according to His will 231

38: THE LORDS PRAYER 232

39: OUR PRAYER, HAIL MARY 235

40: A TRUE TORY OF A LITTLE BOY, CHILD OF GOD 238

41: THE CREATION OF THIS BOOK 241

42: THIS IS THE END OF OUR MAGNIFICENT BEGINNING OF OUR ENDLESS LIVES .. 243

REFERENCES AND FOOTNOTES 245

Your Life's Purpose in God's Grand Design

Introduction

MAGNIFICENT LOVE FROM ALMIGHTY GOD HIMSELF:

This book is an act of magnificent love from our Heavenly Father, our Lord and Savior Jesus Christ, and the Holy Spirit, which proceeds from them. As the apparent author of this book, <u>I say to you that I did not write most of it.</u> This book is not a product of only the theological knowledge I have in my head. I filled in the theological spaces between the major points of Godly information that were directly provided by the Trinity to write this book as described above.

You will certainly notice a tremendous amount of direct text from Almighty God, the Trinity, contained herein. Please understand ***that the text presented in bold italicized letters is information directly from our Creator.*** I am told by the divine that this is the first book of its kind since the Bible, and I am the anointed messenger/author of such divine information since then, in two thousand years.

Yes, it can be accurately said that this book is the first one written in 2,000 years that has God's direct involvement and approval. He wants His exact words communicated outward to all His sacred children in this modern day and age as we draw closer and closer to the end times. This is my task, dear reader, as His messenger.

One hundred percent of this book is specifically designed to greatly assist all God's children to know far more detail about what our magnificent Christian Bible has already said. <u>I am completely flabbergasted and humbled to be His messenger to say the least. He has chosen me</u>. He, our loving Father, put before me a challenging task, to spread His Words to His sacred children, which I will do.

The Divine text written by God looks like this inside this book. This book contains direct divine thoughts communicated to my Christian Spirit regarding new and detailed Biblical Information spoken and inspired by God himself since the last 2,000 years. Take heed of this, my dear

child of God. The words contained in this book are words of God as told to this messenger directly for your benefit.

Your Life's Purpose in God's Grand Design

1

How This Book Came To Be

A STORY OF DIVINE LOVE

Something happened to me on a jet halfway across the Pacific Ocean returning from the Philippines, where my wife and oldest daughter stayed behind in Manila. My sixth spiritual book, "The Divine Resting On My Shoulder," discusses this. I was sitting in my usual window seat, watching the water and clouds go by. Without warning, an absolutely beautiful, magnificent golden orb appeared above the aisle in the jet one row in front

of me. It was ever so bright, emitting magnificently gorgeous rays of beautiful golden light in all directions. It was pulsating as if it was alive. It stayed there for a while, and then it said these words to me, "God loves you!" That was all. I was in my late 20s when this happened. The warmth and the love that the Golden orb sent to me on that day has been with me ever since.

I experienced other such sensations like this when I was delivering healing energy as a Reiki master later on as well. This heralded the beginning of my ever-increasing spiritual life with the sacred Trinity that would grow to magnificent intensity and love as my life continued onward.

Fast-forward to my mid-70s. By now, I have written six Christian spiritual books, all based on my personal experiences. I planned to write a seventh based on my master's degree thesis in theology. The first part of the book was going to be about God's creation. But I soon realized that was such a huge topic it would end up being a book all by itself.

TWO BEAUTIFUL DIVINE SPIRITUAL FIGURES APPEAR TO ME

Then, something magnificent happened. Something that I never would expect. Something that God had planned for me that I had no idea about. After writing about 20 pages or so about God's creation, I started to see, in the distance, off to my right, two beautiful spiritual figures that were perhaps 50 to 70 feet away from me. I knew they were spiritual because, first off, I have seen spiritual figures before. This is nothing new to me because of my past dealings with spiritual entities. Secondly, I could see these figures with either my eyes open or closed.

The spiritual figures were standing there next to each other. One was wearing a white robe, while the other was wearing a white and blue robe. I did not feel uneasy or threatened in any way. In fact, there was an air of peace, contentment, and serene love about them. I was certainly curious.

Two days later, however, I did notice that it seemed both of them have moved a little bit closer to me. Well, that seemed noticeable. Now, this has some of my attention. Life went on, and now I am noticing that with each passing day, these two spiritual figures continue to move closer and closer to me. Each day they became more beautiful. They gave off a wonderful white glow. Additionally, I can see more and more detail about them. When they are only four or five feet from me on my right side, they begin to look like Jesus Christ and our Blessed Mother Mary.

Now I'm thinking to myself, am I preloaded in my mind to see all spiritual figures in this manner? Could I be seeing anybody this way? I didn't want to say anything yet because it is becoming obvious that these two spiritual figures look very much like what we see in the caricatures of our Lord and Savior Jesus Christ and our Blessed Virgin Mary.

About two days later, when I woke up in the morning, both spiritual figures were standing behind my right shoulder, just as if a physical person were standing there. Now there's no denying it. There they were in all their glory. So, I asked them," are you who I think you are? The man said, "Yes, my son, it is I." After that, I don't remember much because my mind went blank.
I will shorten this amazing story about how our Lord and Savior Jesus Christ, and our Blessed Mother approached me to write the book you are

now reading. It is such a heart-warming story to tell. I must have gone into some temporary shock where the thought that our Lord and Savior Jesus Christ was standing right behind my right shoulder and our Blessed Virgin Mary was with Him. What can I possibly say? I had no idea.

After I gathered my senses some unknown time later, I think Jesus said something to the effect that both He and Mother Mary were here to help me with a very important project that my Father in Heaven wants me to do. And, of course, I said yes. It turns out that I said yes to this book you're holding in your hands. I do not remember exactly what He said, frankly. My love for God, for Blessed Mary, and for the Trinity would naturally propel me to say yes to anything they ask of me.

And so, for my dear Christian friend, it is in this way that this book came into being. It is by the express desire of your **Loving Father In Heaven** that this book has been written. Our Lord and Savior, Jesus Christ, has provided so much of the text found within these pages. And it is with our Blessed Holy Mother Mary that has provided details about the birth of our Savior Jesus Christ.

Remember: the words you read are the words spoken by God and only God. And are indicated as such.

This Christian book is the first of its kind. I say this because it contains a large amount of direct detailed revelations to you through your author as a messenger from Almighty God. Everything is very clear in this work. If it is God speaking, *it will always be presented as bold italicized text*. If something comes from my theological or scientific knowledge or a blend of the two, it will be normal text like this.

MY PERSONAL COVENANT WITH ALMIGHTY GOD

Quite some time ago, I entered into a covenant with our Heavenly Father. By then, I had written a number of spiritual books. It became clear that I entered into a position that demanded I always tell the gospel truth of everything in all of my books. I promised our Heavenly Father that I would suffer under the pain of God's punishment if I ever did not. This is my way of showing God my deep love for Him. The book you are reading falls under this covenant, and every word that you read is completely accurate from one to the other. Perhaps this is one of the reasons your Heavenly Father chose me to be His messenger, for this is ever so important material that He wants delivered to all of His sacred children on this earth. Take what He says very seriously, for it will determine your destiny.

The information contained in this book is sorely needed within the Christian community. At this time in the History of mankind, we have never seen so much perversion, hostility, outright lies, and satanic influence throughout all layers of society. This book is an act of love from our Almighty Father in Heaven to reassure all Christians that He remains in total control of our situation today. These days truth is scoffed at, rejected, and attacked by liberals who hate Christianity for the love and the truth it brings to all of God's children.

The situation today is very much that of the Sanhedrin in Jerusalem 2000 years ago, attacking our Lord and Savior Jesus Christ. They felt very threatened, so they illegally had Him crucified. Only today, hatred against Almighty God and Christians is institutionalized within the structure of our American society, entertainment industry, news media, and advertising industry. Everything is now censored to rid our society in America of the truth of things if it does not fit into the liberal agenda of tyrannical socialism.

THE SUBJECT MATTER OF THIS BOOK

There are lots of new information in this book that greatly enhanced our existing Biblical literature. The scope of herein coverage begins uncountable eons of time before the Trinity even thought of creating us their sacred children. Remember God exists in all timelines from the alpha to the omega. It does not end during the magnificent eternal paradise of blissful existence where the Trinity and all of us sacred children delighting together within timeless joy.

Full attribution is given to Almighty God for what He has revealed to me His faithful messenger to the rest of His sacred children. God is the source of all things and the source of all the information contained in this book. This book is completely consistent with our precious Bible and its teachings. This is something that MUST be remembered! It expands on our Biblical traditions and brings new knowledge of what happened even before God's children were created into the Kingdom of Almighty God and born to this earth.

This book contains information from God about what happened eons before creation and why creation became necessary. At one point creation as we know it was NOT necessary. More details on that later on.

This book looks at the crucifixion of our Lord Jesus from His personal point of view because it was He who described it in His experience as written herein. Our Lord and Savior Jesus Christ describes in detail His crucifixion from beginning to end.

This book talks about what happened before the beginning of our universe. It explains why almost all of God's sacred children chose to come to earth and what we are to do here, in other words the purpose of our life. Some chose not to. Their reasons why are contained inside.

This book talks about how and why the spiritual realm, and the physical realm match perfectly with our human bodies. It had to be this way and was so designed by Almighty God to fulfill a specific purpose. It describes how perfectly everything fits together, the spiritual realm, the physical realm, and our two-part bodies. This book gives the purposeful reasons why God created everything this way. Hint, it is for our salvation. That could happen no other way. It is all for us, the salvation of God's sacred children.

This book covers the birth of Jesus as described personally by our Blessed Mother Mary. She gives details that were unknown before this book. Contained herein describes where you and I as God's children were for many eons before we came to earth. It was a magnificent time for all of us. Because all God's children had a choice. Either to come to earth and test ourselves against the temptations of Satan and go back to the Heavenly Kingdom. Or stay in the Heavenly Kingdom and live a wonderful eternal life with some restrictions that our Heavenly Father does not want to place on us. It is our free will choice dear child of God. Either way we are treated with great love and respect.

We all agreed to forgetfulness until we return to the Heavenly Kingdom. Much more new information like this to expand your understanding to greater depths and to cover in awe in fine exquisite details that you never thought existed. That is what this book is about and what our Father in Heaven wants us to know now in this time in our History as His children.

The fate of Satan, all his demons is covered which includes:

- Those who reject Our Holy Trinity by saying things like "I will do things my way".
- Those who follow Satan and wear black clothes etc.,
- Those who do not put others first in their lives, instead, live only for themselves.
- Those who commit crimes, sexual crimes, irresponsibility etc.
- Those who violate the commandments handed down by Moses.
- Those are narcissistic, very self-centered, use other people for self-gain, manipulate other people and lastly want to control other people.

It is these people that will not participate in the glorious Kingdom that is yet to come. It sadly is these of God's sacred children that will be with Satan and his demons that will populate hell as it slowly disintegrates through ever increasing entropy that will force all matter to ultimately evaporate into nothingness. It is from nothingness they came from and it is to nothingness which they shall return.

MY DIVINE PURPOSE

Our Holy Father has asked me to write His exact thoughts and words that contain extensive new knowledge of Christianity. It is designed completely for God's sacred children on earth today in our History. I must emphasize that 100% of this Biblical literature is completely consistent with both the Old and New Testaments. There are no contradictions. None.

Rather what you are going to read extends the Bible. This book begins eons before the Bible begins. How can this be? It is because Almighty God provided all the accurate information. It is the divine who spoke through me, our Father's Anointed Messenger, word for word to reveal to you God's sacred children all that is perfect and holy for our time in human history. I am also to ensure that His words and thoughts are published in a very elegant manner. This entire effort is for every child of God on this planet. God loves each of us, so very much it goes beyond our understanding and imagination. If I sound redundant, it is because I purposely am. In no way does this book replace any part of the Bible. It never will and is never intended to do that in any way. This book brings much more detail and extended understanding of the Bible and the life and times of our Lord and Savior, Jesus Christ.

FOR CLARITY'S SAKE

Separating God's Words From Mine

The thoughts and words revealed to me from; Almighty God, our Lord and Savior Jesus Christ, or our Blessed Holy Mother Mary have been presented in bold and italicized type within quotes so you may easily see their words as separate from mine. ***Their words are always bold and italicized.***

God's Astonishing Statement To Me:

I have a personal covenant with our Father to be a fountain of truth in His name on this earth. To publish all that our Father in Heaven wants His children to know about at this time in History. During one of my deep prayerful and meditative sessions with our Father in Heaven, He told me the following words. Yes, these are our Father's exact words given to me to publish for all His children.

A NOTE FROM ALMIGHTY GOD:

"You are the first that I am allowing to speak with Me directly and let that be written. You are a unique child of mine and I am very pleased."
August 17, 2022, 03.23 PM

I was completely astonished to hear God say this to me personally. I never thought or imagined that something like this would happen to me. Yet, it certainly did. As you read through the rest of this book, there are many times that Almighty God in the Trinity answered my specific questions. Inspect the content of what is said and get a feel of the authority behind the words. Ask yourself whether a human being could make this stuff up. Look at the information that is provided. All of it is consistent with the Bible. The pre-existing covenant with Almighty God is simple. I will always tell His Truth without fail, without omission. Failure to do so will result in the wrath of our Father, whom I love so very much.

You Have A Decision To Make Dear Child Of God

You have free will, as God has given it to all of us. You are free to choose your reaction to the above statement from Almighty God. This is your choice through free will. Either accept this as I have said or reject it now. Your decision will be chronicled in the Akashic records of all mankind.

<u>Now, the decision is yours to believe this or not</u>. As in all things theological and in faith, it is up to you to decide in your heart if this book is from Almighty God or if it is something from a horrific illusion perpetrated by Satan and written by a wacko religious nut. It is pretty much that simple.

Almighty God is my witness.

Blessings. Your child of God author, Richard Ferguson

MY FATAL SICKNESS

If we get sick, our Heavenly Father has the power to intervene, if necessary, according to our Father's plan for us. God's presence is inside us and may heal us from fatal diseases according to his will. I know personally for certain that this is true.

According To the Will Of Our Heavenly Father

My darling wife of 38 years died of cancer after having her life extended by our loving Father in Heaven through what I did for her in daily deep prayerful Reiki healing sessions. Her life was extended from 18 months to five years by our Father in Heaven because of the Reiki sessions I performed for her every day. Many years later, it was Jesus Christ that told me this. My late wife also told me this. Yes, she is in Heaven and still loves me very much, as I love her too.

Sometime later, I developed a fatal cancer that many men can be afflicted with to one degree or another. I got it big time. I had no symptoms at all.

My darling fiancée had been bugging me to get a physical for a few years. I was sick of doctors, having gone through so many of them with Marilyn's cancer, and the last thing I needed was another doctor. She finally convinced me to go. Well, the worst did happen.

When I was diagnosed, it was normally too late for people like me. I had no symptoms. But it was already fatal when I found out that I had it. I had terminal prostate cancer.

The bad number was anything above 10. I wish mine was near that. It was big multiples way gone above that. During the previous five years, I gave my total attention to my wife, who had terminal cancer. I ignored myself completely and gave my darling wife my complete full attention.

I had no idea I had cancer. I did not have any symptoms. Years later, my fiancée convinced me to get a checkup. She is the best loving woman in the universe! After many radiation treatments, I glowed in the dark, so to speak. Now, I am out of the woods. Cancer free. To say I glowed in the dark is not as big of an exaggeration as you might think.

Years later, God our Loving Father told me it **was his will that I will survive.** I will tell you a sacred secret that Jesus Christ told me recently.

What Healing Really Is According To Our Lord And Savior Jesus Christ?

He said that *the miracle of healing is really a very accelerated process of the body's normal healing. Each of us has built-in your physical bodies and immensely complex immunological system that kills disease. Healing is what it means. It kills off that which would terminate life. In your case, my dear son, it was the will of your Father to extend your life and so we did by simply greatly amplifying your natural healing processes within your body. The treatment you got from your doctor certainly helped a great deal also. Your doctors were very good at what they did.*

The Will of God Intervenes In My Behalf And Heals Me

My treatments were successful, and my doctors were amazed. Later, my doctor told me on several occasions that **I had "outside help"** in my healing, meaning it was more than just medicine that saved my life. He should know. He deals with this disease every day. Because God healed me, now I can write you this most important book. I know for certain that Almighty God wants me to publish this book. How? Because He told me so.

You have a decision to make

So, my fellow Christian, if you are ever looking for a person that God healed, you certainly can use my name. I should have died, so says my doctors, and so says Almighty God. You cannot get better testimony than that. Additionally, were it not for my healing, you would not be reading this book. And, to think that I had no symptoms. I should listen to my wife more often.

2

The Heavenly Spiritual World Today

IN THE BEGINNING

For all of us sacred children of God, it is impossible to understand where this book begins. It begins with the testimony of our Almighty Father in the Heavenly Kingdom when He describes a timeless time when only the Trinity existed in luxurious ecstasy, exploring the infinite other— exploring the magnificent infinite dimensions of each other with limitless love and grandeur. Then at some point in timeless time, the three decided they wanted to share what they had with their own sacred children made in their image. And so that would come to be. And so, the beginning … Began!

3

A Chronology of Events

The Trinity as One

Throughout the dimensionless and timeless time, there was only three,
there was the Trinity.
Their existence ever so blissful, peaceful to see yet powerful to be.
in countless facets of diamond like beauty, love was complete.
An existence shimmering, infinite extensions, endless possibilities.
So ever brilliant shining across eons of time sparkling endless thoughts.
That if We wished would become real objects for further study and joy.
Trinity infinite indeed, exploring the other, no end ever to that.
Which was, ecstasy, a glorious beginningless beginning!
An endless end of that some dear sacred children you will see.
Of Our deep enjoyment, unmeasurable belovedness you will also see.

Chronology of events as understood in relation to the passage of time within both the spiritual realm and the physical realm that we, as God's sacred children, would experience.

God exists eternally outside of time, a timeless time, across many multiple dimensions, far more than we are aware of and understand. The Trinity was, is, and always will exist outside of time and the physical and spiritual worlds that are yet to come. Before the creation that we know of that we call the creation of the beginning.

The creation of the Angels occurred an unmeasurable amount of eons prior to the decision to create His sacred angels. They exist inside the Heavenly Kingdom to serve Almighty God. More angels will be created by our Heavenly Father in order to serve His purposes in the larger spiritual realm and His sacred children going forward after they are created and spend eons of time with Almighty God in the Heavenly Kingdom.

Upon deciding to create His sacred children made in His image, God prepared the way for His children by creating many more angels to serve as messengers and more between His children and himself. They will also serve as guardian angels to protect His sacred children from the yet-to-come Satan and His demons.

Eons before the Trinity thought of creating children in their image, God certainly already knew of Lucifer's plan to rebel against Him. Remember, our Almighty Father exists across all time, the Alpha and the Omega. So, in addition to creating more angels to serve His yet-to-be-created children, God also creates both the spiritual and physical realms that will contain the earth. It is the earth that will host His sacred children when they are to decide where they want to spend eternity. This is where God created our universe and all the laws that surrounded it. The same is true for the spiritual realm. Both of these realms are created tailor-made to perfection to match the needs of us sacred children while we are here on earth. The spiritual realm matches our interior spirit and minds so we can communicate with the divine. The physical realm matches perfectly with the needs of our bodies so we may live on the earth long enough to decide our eternal destiny.

Said differently, God creates it in anticipation of the dual nature of His now-existing sacred spiritual children. They will have physical bodies so as to procreate across the ages allowing more and more of His sacred spiritual children the opportunity to live with Him for all eternity in paradise. Now Almighty God also has a place to send Lucifer after His coming unsuccessful rebellion along with one-third of the angelic realm.

It is then that Lucifer falls in love with himself, and through pride and arrogance, he attempts to usurp God's rightful throne. War begins in Heaven, and Lucifer becomes Satan, the adversary, and is thrown down to the pre-existing spiritual realm outside of the Heavenly Kingdom and to the physical realm, where he becomes the prince of earth. In human time, the war between Almighty God and Lucifer with his cadre of fallen angels concludes within a blink of an eye. Lucifer never did have any chance and was thrown out of the Heavenly Kingdom.

As part of the spiritual realm, Almighty God creates a special place that is sealed off from the rest of the spiritual realm. This is the place where Satan and his demons will govern. They will govern over all of God's children who purposely rejected God during their life on earth. At this point, everything is now prepared for the coming rebellion of Lucifer and one-third of the angelic host.

Satan appears to Eve as a wise serpent and lies to her that they would become like God if they ate the fruit from the tree of the knowledge of good and evil. Eating from this tree was specifically forbidden by Almighty God. Adam and Eve blatantly disobey their Father by eating from the forbidden tree of the knowledge of good and evil. Because of this, they were thrown out of the garden where life was so excellent as intended by God.

From that point onward, all mankind becomes separated from Almighty God and must now grovel in the dirt to sustain themselves and all their future children. From this point onwards, the Christian Bible and associated Biblical literature describe in detail what happens next, including the offer of redemption made possible by the painful sacrifice and death of God's only begotten Son Jesus Christ. Only after our Lord and Savior's sacrifice and ascension into Heaven can we, God's sacred children, say yes to God's offer of eternal life in paradise with Him.

From this point on, all of God's sacred children who come to earth's physical realm now participate in spiritual warfare. We Christians must fight against the completely hateful group of demons led by princes and principalities of the satanic realm. All of the hate-filled destruction on earth emanates from the sealed-off part of the spiritual realm called hell. To clarify, Satan and his demons are spiritual beings and have some access to the general spiritual realm. They use this to destroy whatever they can that is created by God. This allows them to deceive as many of God's sacred children as possible. Once a child of God thoroughly rejects our Almighty Father upon their physical death, they will go to the hell pre-prepared by our Heavenly Father for those who do so.

This leads us to summarize the situation we have today on earth. However, remember that this tawdry and painful situation on earth will not last much longer. Almighty God will bring the physical earth to a close in the not-too-distant future. Also, our Lord and Savior Jesus Christ will return to this earth to establish love and peace among all that dwell here. With this, I will end this extremely shortened history.

4

Our Magnificent Story Begins

Many eons ago, as we think of it, there was a timeless time when all that existed was the Holy Trinity. The totality of everything we know of was the sacred Holy Trinity. Each of the three was infinite and limitless in all ways that they chose to be. Each was and eternally powerful beyond imagination. Their existence was complete ecstasy, happiness and fulfillment. Their joy and complete fulfillment came with the endless exploration of each other's infinite character, power, and personality. The Trinity needed nothing as they each were complete in and of themselves. And if they so wanted, they could expand outward their exploits in any manner they chose to continue their fulfillment and joy. As children of God, we cannot begin to understand or fathom the extent of their infinite love for each other and their limitless power.

The fact that the holy Trinity knows each of us so intimately is a fact of all creation. To those who reject our loving Almighty Father, this is absolutely horrifying for they rely on keeping secrets to themselves. Problem is that nothing and no one can hide from our Almighty Father. They have rejected God and given themselves over to Satan and his demons. Somehow, they think no one will find out what their evil deeds and thoughts and motivations are. This complete and detailed perfect knowledge of everything a child of God has said and done and the motivations behind it will be used when each child has his life review after they die. Jesus Christ and powerful angels will be there in a very loving environment. They could not be more wrong if they think they have gotten away with things. Absolutely everything is known and out in the open. There is absolutely nothing that can be hidden in the universe from anybody. Nothing!

The opposite is true about those of God's sacred children who love the Trinity. The holy Trinity knows absolutely everything about each of God's children including all the activity within their minds and absolutely everything they do and the motivations behind that. For the sacred children who consciously choose the ways of our heavenly father, this news brings great joy. Each of us can now understand that the heavenly Trinity knows everything about our lives, our sufferings, our health, and all activities we engage in while on the earth. These sacred children who have constantly chosen the ways of God and expressed their love of our Heavenly Father, our Lord and Savior Jesus Christ, and the Holy Spirit which proceeds from them, for them their life review will be a very pleasant and loving experience before they are allowed into the eternal kingdom of God.

At one moment within this timeless time before creation, the Trinity thought it would be a magnificent idea to create special and sacred children in their image. And so, they did. We are all created by the limitless loving Trinity, the Father, the only begotten Son, and the Holy Spirit, which proceeds from them. We, as their children, were given some limited powers of the Holy Trinity, but most importantly, we were given the power to love and to communicate with our Holy Almighty Father, his only begotten Son, and the Holy Spirit.

Our Holy Trinity loves you and me so much that the Father designed the creation of his children and the realms in which we live so that they are within the very core of our physical and spiritual being. In this way, they can experience everything we do while we exist on earth and elsewhere. Whatever it is we experience in our lives, the Trinity also experiences. From my personal life, our Father, his Son, and the Holy Spirit are so wonderfully intertwined within each of us that they know our thoughts, emotions, motivations, and who and what we love. The Holy Trinity knows every detail within our minds, everything we say and do while on this earth, and even every detail of our physical bodies.

SECRETS, THEY ARE IMPOSSIBLE

There are absolutely no secrets within the spiritual realm, nor should there ever be, for our Father is not like that in any way. Said differently, our Father in Heaven is not limited in any way throughout all of his creations. Like what Psalm 139 says, "no matter where I go, you dear Father, you are always there. "

I must say to everybody that it is impossible for the cosmos or any other part of creation to contain any secret anywhere. Everything is just transparent. This comes as a big surprise for all the crooks on earth when they die and have their life reviewed.

THE TIME WE SPENT WITH GOD IN HEAVEN

You and I are the sacred spiritual children of Almighty God, our Holy Father, who loves every one of us. After our Father created all his children, for an undetermined length of time, all of us would stay with the Trinity in the Heavenly Kingdom. We stayed with the Holy Trinity for unknown eons of time as we would measure it today. It is here that we children would be nurtured, loved, explore the Heavenly realm, and play with our Almighty Father in so many different ways. We also learned about the values given by our Father. This includes all his characteristics and personality and his unlimited love.

This gave our Father infinite joy and happiness to be with His children. Additionally, this was a time within the Kingdom of Heaven to learn about our Almighty Father before we were born into the physical earth. We were to learn about His creation, learn about ourselves, and mature in the direction of the talents and personal characteristics that our Father intended for each of us. Remember, each child is individually unique. No two are the same.

We learned about ourselves and all creation inside the Heavenly realm and outside it as well. We played games with our loving Father. He nurtured us and told us wonderful stories about the creation to come. It was a wonderland of delight, joy, happiness, and fulfillment, especially when our Father would teach us about the many delightful things yet to come. Our Father's sacred children were happy beyond human description when we would play with Him and frolic and enjoy with all the other children in the Heavenly Kingdom. All of us matured in different ways, none the same, all different as was the will of our Father.

Over what we now call time, each child grew in different ways from all the others. Each one of us was becoming a unique one-of-a-kind individual child of God. God does not ever use a cookie-cutter in any of his creations, no matter what it may be.

Remember that Almighty God exists independent of time. He knows what will happen in the future in great detail because He is already living there. He is the Alpha and Omega. God knew well in advance of Satan's coming rebellion. Therefore, as a supreme act of love for his children, God created the spiritual and physical realms, which would overlap each other. It must be this way because God created his sacred children with two parts, the spiritual part, which exists in our minds, and the physical part, which allows his children to procreate and provide a pathway for their salvation that leads directly back to God in Heaven and eternal life with our Father.

<u>The reason for all creation is a monumental act of love for God's children. It is to use this pathway back to the origin of their existence in the Heavenly realm and life with our Heavenly Father for all eternity.</u>

GOD'S CHILDREN MUST MAKE A CHOICE

For our loving Father had known all so well that one of his angels
Would rebel, admired his beauty, lusted God's throne, was compelled.
And so, he did, futile at best. One third the angelic host expelled.
All this war done in a blink of an eye; we were not yet created.
In a blink of an eye now Satan thrown down, hell is what was waited.
Fully one third of the heavenly angelic host also cast aside.
Into the hellish abode, them never to return but seething outside.

For them the spiritual realm will be their temporary playground
Havoc they will create, awful evil, eye for eye and pound for pound.
Their angelic powers stripped away, though thoughts they cast around.
Ugly they are, misfigured, so much hate, distorted creatures of sin.
They look like something thrown into the garbage bin.
Satan banished, his ugly demons too, down to a pit made just for them.

We were all aware that we would be born into the physical realm and live our lives according to the will of God. But He never forces anything upon us because He gave us our free will. Here on the earth, we would live for a short time to choose which path we would take, by how we show our love and actions toward others of God's children, we will be choosing either Heaven or hell by our own free will.

Lastly, before we were born into the physical, we had to pass through the process of forgetting. We could not take with us to earth all that we were taught and experienced in the Heavenly realm. That would stay behind us until we returned to our Father in Heaven. To make a pure choice of our destiny, we had to leave behind the experiences and knowledge we gained in Heaven.

Our choice is exceedingly difficult yet very simple. Choose our Almighty Father and his ways, or choose Satan and his lawless evil. The second choice allows everyone to run wild with no attention to the laws of Almighty God. One path leads toward Almighty God and eternal life in paradise. The  other path leads toward irreversible separation from our Father and ultimate death through the complete dissolution of existence and back into nothingness. For God created his sacred children out of nothingness, and for those who reject God, they will return back into nothingness. This is the second death as described four times in the book of Revelation written by the apostle John. Revelation 2:11, 20:6, 20:14 and lastly Revelation 21:8. *"But the cowardly, unbelieving, abominable, murderers, sexually immoral, sorcerers, idolaters, and all liars shall have their part in the lake which burns with fire and brimstone, which is the* **second death.***"*

This choice is demonstrated for all eternity by how we conduct our spiritual and physical lives on earth. Each child demonstrates their choice by living their lives according to God's laws and God's love for each other…or not! All of creation watches and observes our behavior and how we choose, for there are no hidden secrets within all of God's creation. This is so even if some children think they are able to hide something. All criminals think this is true, that they can hide things. They are wrong. It is impossible by God's design to keep hidden anything within his creation.

God's children would need to make this choice during their lives on earth, where Satan has access to them because the physical and spiritual realms overlap each other. Also, remember that all of God's sacred children are part spiritual and part physical. Our spiritual part gives God's children direct access to their Father in Heaven.

This is true even if it is not understood or perceived. But also, it gives Satan the opportunity to influence all of us children to reject Almighty God. This gives every child of God the opportunity to affirm their love for our Father or choose Satan and his hell leading to their dissolution into nothingness. Lastly, God already knows how each child will choose their destiny before they make their decision. Why? Again, it is because God has no limitations and exists independent of time.

One by one, God's sacred children would be born into this spiritual and physical realm using the human bodies that their Father and the rest of the Trinity had designed for us to occupy with our spiritual being. Our bodies on earth were designed by God to perfectly match the spiritual and physical realms that their loving Father designed for them. It was this combination of the two realms with the two parts of the human body. Their minds and spirit allowed God's children to communicate with their Father in Heaven.

Their physical is to demonstrate their choice for choosing their Father in Heaven and eternal life or Satan and ultimate disintegration into nothingness. Of course, it is within their minds and spirits that their choice is made. But their physical body demonstrates their choice through their behavior on earth. When God's only begotten Son, Jesus Christ, came to earth, He spelled out very clearly what the choice was for God's children, all of them.

Unknown to us children, their first two parents on this earth, Adam and Eve, made a grave error by disobeying our Almighty Father. Against God's explicit instructions, they ate from the tree of the knowledge of good and evil. They gave in to the lies of Satan posing as a snake. This permanently stained our first two parents with sin and all their human descendants that would be born on planet Earth. And so, this is the heritage of all human beings on planet earth.

5

The Heavenly Realm

THE HEAVENLY KINGDOM

I consider myself to be a typical Christian. And being a Christian, I have had many questions about the nature and characteristics of Heaven. We all have heard many stories about this that and the other thing regarding Heaven. It is also described in the Bible. But I wanted to use my very close, loving relationship with Almighty God to explore the truth of what Heaven is. This is not comprehensive by any means, but it does shed a lot of light on our understanding of the Heavenly realm. It is a given that Heaven is a spiritual place and not a physical one. First, here are a few representations from Biblical literature that describe our Heavenly destiny.

In the books of Genesis, Exodus, Leviticus, Deuteronomy, and all the other Old Testament books, Heaven is described as "all that is above the earth and where the stars are." A very basic and fundamental understanding.

In the New Testament, starting with the book of Matthew, Heaven takes on a different identity. Matthew refers to Heaven as "the Kingdom of Heaven." It also becomes the place where our Father, Almighty God, comes from. It is the home of God within the Kingdom of Heaven. It is also the dwelling place for the Son of man, meaning Lord Jesus Christ and the Angels as described in the gospel of Mark.

It was also the home for Lucifer, the angel, until he rebelled against God and fell like lightning from Heaven in the book of Luke. In Hebrews, Heaven is also characterized as a sanctuary. In the book of Revelation, Heaven is also characterized as the source of Godly power, grace, and everlasting joy for those who accept Almighty God's love.

SOME DETAILED QUESTIONS ABOUT THE HEAVENLY KINGDOM

With all of this in mind, I had a number of questions that I would love to have our Heavenly Father give us further knowledge about.
My questions were:

- Has the Heavenly realm been in existence for eternity like the Holy Trinity?
- What are some details of the Heavenly realm? Describe the realm of Almighty God.
- What is its size relative to the spiritual realm and the physical realm?
- How are its borders protected from evil, from Satan and his demons?
- Is there only one entrance, or gate, that allows entry into the Heavenly realm?

I sat down with my laptop and meditated on these questions about Heaven. I prayed to our Lord in Heaven and asked if He would respond, knowing I would publish this in my seventh book. God answered my prayer with such warmth and love, and his revelation and words are below. You are holding the only book in Christian literature that has permission from Almighty God that receives revelations from Him, and the author is allowed to print that for the benefit of his sacred children.

With all this in mind, we have come to this book's particularly important and interesting section. That is, with the help of Almighty God, it is to describe what Heaven is like. We know it is far different than this Satan-drenched earth we live in now. As time goes on, circumstances on earth are only getting worse and worse. So let us concentrate on what our Christian future is.

ALMIGHTY GOD ANSWERS THE QUESTIONS ABOVE
July 30, 2022, 5:28 PM

My dear children, the Trinity has always lived in the Heavenly realm. It has no beginning; it exists now and will live on. It is eternal where what you call time in the physical realm does not exist. Heaven is all around you whether you realize it or not. Heaven is also a place. Within this realm there are different forms of life that exist, of course us within the Trinity, Almighty God our Father, myself which is His only begotten Son and the Holy Spirit which precedes from us within the Trinity outward to the other realms of existence.

And that includes of course our sacred children made in our image. Size wise which is something our children can relate to, Heaven has no outer boundaries and within it, it contains all the other spiritual realms that you have described within this magnificent book. As you know my son, we within the Trinity are pure spiritual beings that encompass the entire realm of what you call Heaven. Again, it is infinite in all of the multiple dimensions that your scientists are working on, and it contains all the different time dimensions as well.

It is exceedingly easy for us within the Trinity to use all these different dimensions of space, time, and other aspects of dimensionality to serve us in the Trinity to explore an infinite different variety of attributes, qualities, intense love from each of us in the Trinity back to the others.

Within your book dear son, you are exploring the characteristics and nature of the physical realm, the spiritual realm and now the Heavenly realm. There are other realms but none of those pertain to your existence within our divine goals for you, our children. We within the Trinity are easily able to create more dimensions and more realms of existence if we so choose and that serves our purpose.

Remember all that is needed is a thought to bring something into existence and it is done. What you call Heaven has been our home from before eternity began. I know to you that sounds like an oxymoron, but it is not. Considering all the different dimensions that we have created that you are unaware of, that statement is not understandable.

Yet, it is true. You asked about defining in more detail what the Heavenly realm is like. It is not like the physical realm or in the spiritual realm that you currently reside in. Its laws of physics for example are very much different than those on earth within the physical realm. There is far more freedom to come and go as you wish without any effort on your part. All you need to do is think about where you want to be and you may will it for you to be there.

All communications within our sacred children and the Angels and of course us within the Trinity are as you would call telepathic. That is not to say that there is no sound in the Heavenly realm, it is quite the opposite. Your Lord Father in Heaven loves to hear the angels sing and He loves to hear the voices of his children such as yourself. If you cannot sing on earth, that is certainly not a problem for you will be surprised at how deliciously wonderful you will sound in the Heavenly realm.

Angels will come and go and be with you as your constant companion if you wish. All of you will know each other and their histories of each other and their struggles on earth if that is what you wish. The depth of love that you will feel within the Heavenly realm is far more intense and pleasurable than you can imagine.

My son, I know you remember the golden orb that appeared to you on the jet halfway across the Pacific Ocean. That is when you were told the following words, "God loves you". Along with that simple message came a magnificently intense feeling of love for you. I know you felt like running up and down the aisle of the jet proclaiming that God loves us. It is good that you chose not to for that would have created such an incident of confusion among the other people that it would not be good for them.

As I said earlier on the realms of existence are contained within the Heavenly realm. But this does not mean in any way things cannot flow into and out from the Heavenly realm without strong conditions and protection from Satan and his demons. The Heavenly realm with all its different physics and roles of spirituality is completely fortified from any intrusion from those spirits that do not belong there no matter how small the intrusion might be.

Within the Heavenly realm there are different layers of existence. There are seven layers to be exact and each of the ascending layers, become filled with more and more gratification, fulfillment, intensifying love, and other rewards that are consistent with what each of our children has shown themselves to be while they are on the earth.

Remember my son that the creation of the physical realm and the spiritual realm is matched perfectly with the design of your human body. This is so the needs of your physical body are met with the resources available to you on earth. And as I said before, it is your brain and the overlying spiritual body that you have that is completely in tune with the spiritual realm.

Many people have speculated on the size of the Holy Kingdom where God Almighty resides and where the Holy Spirit and myself call home. All of our creations are from our Heavenly realm. Your Father so loves his children that not only after you were thought into existence, all being individually different from every other, you lived with your Father in Heaven as spiritual beings for a long time. This is so He could enjoy each of you personally and love you in the ways that match your talents, your attributes, your characteristics and what has been decided would be the trajectory of your life once you are born on earth.

What your Biblical literature says about the details of which God knows each of you when it says Almighty God even knows the number of hairs on your head, this is so true. For Almighty God, resides not only in around and through all of creation but we also know every detail of your life, your motivations, and everything you say and do. For it is in this way that we are able to separate the sheep from the goats. There are no secrets within all of creation.

The size of the Heavenly Kingdom is on purpose smaller than what I described Heaven to be. For the Heavenly Kingdom where we in the Trinity reside necessarily is smaller. Yet for our children that join us within the Heavenly realm eternally, it will seem unending in every way. There will be no restrictions upon the children of God. Yet at the same time there will be some responsibilities for each of our sacred children, however this is a very light load for the Heavenly realm is meant to be a paradise for all of our Father's children.

Our children will have all of creation at their feet to explore and be in wonderment of what their Heavenly Father created for them. Remember all of creation that you see in the Heavens above and this bears within you and other things are specifically designed to create a pathway from the wreckage in your minds that have been caused by Lucifer now known as Satan and all of his demons.

If there is, as some of your poets have said, a key to the gates of Heaven it can be simply stated as belief and faith in me as your Lord and Savior, love in your hearts for all your fellow children of God.

You asked about how is the Kingdom of God in Heaven protected from those who do not belong. There are a number of ways that this is accomplished but you will not understand them. But one way that you will is the  *many very powerful angels that we have that are able to keep things well in order based on the will of your Father.*

Is there one gate to the entrance of Heaven? Yes, my son there is one path to the Heavenly realm and there is one gate and one gate only. Only those found in the book of life as you call it and that have kept the word of your Father in Heaven, love others of his children as you love yourself and the commandments given by God to Moses.

It is only those that find their names in the sacred book. And as you and I have discussed before, only the few will find their names written in this book of life. There are many more things I could tell you my dear son but I believe this will answer your questions and the understandings of the nature of existence by all of your readers that decide to take the time and effort to read the words contained in this magnificent book you have written with of course the help we give you from the Trinity. I love you my dear son.

The preceding three pages is a combination of questions answered by our loving Lord and Savior, Jesus Christ, over a period of time spanning a month or two.

Dear Reader:
I think that you should make an effort to study in detail the above revelation from Almighty God. And then compare them with the appropriate verses in the Bible. You will immediately find out that this book offers great details that our Bible does not have. This book covers areas earlier than the Old Testament and Beyond Revelation. First, if you did this, you would have a marvelous understanding of the different characteristics of different realms created by the Trinity. You would know a lot about the relationships between the different areas of creation.

There is a wealth of knowledge in the above revelation from one of the members of the Trinity. In doing this, your faith and understanding of all things Christian will be expanded and deepened. Also, you will benefit from a vastly improved closeness and understanding of the Trinity itself.

The information that I have presented to you is priceless. This information does not exist anywhere else within the Christian world. Read it, absorb it, and study it. You will have to do this on your own because I do not believe any parish priest would be able to comment on this theological material. As for me, I do understand all of this because of my experience throughout my life. I have had mystical experiences almost every day since I was 25 years old. Having a master's degree in theology and pastoral ministry, chemistry, physics, quantum physics, astronomy, and so on is of enormous help.

Additionally, having been a scientist at NASA is necessary to understand how God created our universe with incredible precision. This information appears in a different place in this book. The collective result of these sciences prove that our universe was purposely designed and crafted with an impossible amount of precision necessary for our universe to function and support human life.

Lastly, and as a reminder, you are holding a gold mine of truth that originated from our Almighty Father in Heaven. I hope and pray that reading this book will bring you far closer to our Father. This is through understanding more about the magnificent extent of the realms He has created so we may join Him again in the Kingdom of Heaven. There we will experience wondrous joy and love with Him with no restrictions on us to explore and exemplify our love for our Father in Heaven.

MORE QUESTIONS FOR ALMIGHTY GOD

After a number of weeks had passed from the revelation that God has provided for his children that read this book, I developed some more questions that I want to ask Almighty God our Father about the Heavenly realm and God's sacred children who now live there. They are as follows:

Can you please describe whether or not a sacred child can advance to higher levels within the Heavenly realm after they are already there? I know our Father continually encourages additional growth, understanding, and learning. So, there must be opportunities for us as children to do this while in Heaven. Am I correct?

In the above answers to my initial questions, you stated, **"Within this realm** (the Heavenly)**, there are different forms of life that exist."** You mentioned some of them we already know about. However, are there others? It would not be surprising to me that since the Trinity is infinite, there would be many other forms of life.

Dear Lord, you mentioned the following, which surprised me. **Heaven has no outer boundaries, and within it, it contains all the other spiritual realms.** I never thought of Heaven as containing all the other realms. Does this mean that the Heavenly realm overlaps in some manner all other realms? Is Heaven integrated with the other realms? Or are they in some fashion side-by-side except for the spiritual realm overlapping with the physical realm so God's sacred children can employ their spiritual minds and physical bodies?

Does this also mean that the Heavenly realm contains the realm we call hell? In the gospel of Luke, He describes Lucifer as being cast down and out of Heaven, and he became Satan, the prince of the earth. This terminology of up-and-down indicates that there may be some dimensionality within the Heavenly realm. Is this correct?

On a different note, because this question just occurred to me, my dear Almighty God, Creator of all things seen and unseen, what is your definition of "life"? I have my own definition, but my definition does not count. It is your definition and description that is of supreme importance. I would love to know, and I believe all your sacred children also want to know about this answer.

There are no secrets within all of creation. You mentioned this in the text above. This comes as no surprise. However, would you, dear Lord, go into more detail regarding the impossibility of secrets within creation? Also, what are the reasons that creation is this way?

Yet for our children that join us within the Heavenly realm eternally, it will seem unending in every way. There will be no restrictions upon the children of God.

I have a practical example and question for you. As a pilot with a commercial license, does this mean that I, in some manner unknown to me be able to fly my favorite airplane, a Boeing 747, from San Francisco to Paris inside the Heavenly Kingdom? Okay, I know this is a nutty question, but it's a good example of stretching what I believe are the Holy characteristics of the Heavenly realm. Yes, dear Lord, you can tease me on this one. I can hear you laughing already.

ANSWERS FROM OUR LORD JESUS CHRIST
August 22, 2022, 11.20 AM

Oh, my dear child, you have certainly posed very interesting and pertinent questions that will benefit our sacred children. Thank you for asking them of me. Regarding your question about advancing to higher levels when a child is already in the Heavenly Kingdom, the answer is most certainly yes. And yes, you are correct that your Father encourages working and learning more and more about not only yourself but also everything that exists around you. And learning, you will automatically be increasing your ability to love and to help others of those in Heaven more deeply and thoroughly. This is by giving of yourself to all others of God's children. This will result in an ever-increasing amount of reward for those of our children that put forth the effort.

Yes, my dear son, there are other forms of life within the created realms that your Father has done. However, they have no impact on your lives and the trajectory of your existence. The best word to describe this is that you are separated from other forms of life. This is a very good thing because having knowledge of other forms of life necessarily means that you will be exposed to the knowledge of different sets of the laws of physics, different situations that these other kinds of children of God are dealing with completely separate from your own. Everything about any other kinds of children of God are very foreign and almost always from your existence. Hence, there is no benefit for you to know anything about the other dimensions, the other forms of life. If you did know something, it would be detrimental to your spiritual path back to us in the Trinity and especially your infinite loving Almighty Father.

Regarding the size of the Heavenly realm, it is true that the Heavenly realm has no boundaries. It encompasses and supersedes all other realms. It must be this way because the Holy Trinity has access to all realms and is present in every particle of existence and all realms. All of this points to the creation of a pathway for all of God's sacred children back to Him in the Heavenly Kingdom which basically means their redemption. The Heavenly Kingdom is relatively small and has extremely fortified and protected boundaries around it in all directions so that there cannot be even the slightest incursion that is not permitted by our very strict laws of entry.

First, this is a very profound question. It is fundamental to all existence. What the Trinity means by the word "life" and all of God's children as well, means that there must be certain characteristics and attributes to a being that exists in the spiritual realm and or the physical realm. Within the spiritual realm there is abundant life featured by a separate identity from all others. A separate life means an individual and separate will, a separate point of view when perceiving the reality around it, being able to communicate with others of its kind as a separate entity and being perceived as a separate entity from others of its kind. There must be a certain minimum level of intelligence and reasoning power. There must be a memory and it must follow certain rules of behavior that govern its actions in the environment in which it lives. Their life must be able to form relationships with others of its kind participating in group activities but also having the ability to act alone. It must be sentient absorbing information regarding its environment and other forms of life. It must be able to make decisions based on experience, memory and environmental information and even instinct and habit patterns. It must be able to act to preserve its own survival. These are a few of the characteristics that earmark a life in the physical realm. The spiritual realm is different.

Regarding the fact that nothing can be hidden within all creation this is the manner in which your Almighty Father decided to design all creation. Think of what it would be like if this were not true. Within the sphere of God's children or human life if there was no such thing as truth or having the natural flow be earmarked by unknown secrets, there would be no cultures there would be no societies, it would not be possible to have loving relationships because loving relationships are built on knowing the other person in detail. There would always be rightful suspicion of anyone and everybody in all circumstances. Society would simply cease to function even in the simplest interpersonal transactions.

The human justice systems are based on the discovery of what defendants are hiding and trying to keep secret. Without the exposure of truth there would be no justice in society and victims of crime would not have any recourse against perpetrators that cause damage in one way or another. Simply put there can be  *no secrets. The decision at what you call judgment day is based upon knowing every little detail of each child of God. This means not only knowing the actions of a person but also the emotions, the motivations, the intentions, and other factors that play inside the spirit and mind of the human person.*

Almost everybody does not know or understand that within the human mind there are no secrets from God. Absolutely everything is revealed and known by the Trinity. This is what is used to make a completely fair decision regarding the eternal future of every child of God.
I love this question of yours dear son.

Leave it to you to come up with an extremely entertaining yet complex example of the dimensionality for the Heavenly Kingdom. This tells me that you do understand about how the Heavenly Kingdom exists within the Heavenly realm. I know that some of your most happy moments in your life on earth was in an airplane doing all sorts of things that only a very seasoned and experienced pilot could do.

The answer to your question is of course yes. For that matter, if you wished you could take one of the airplanes you owned and fly them to the moon. Remember dear son, there are no limitations in the Heavenly Kingdom. Knowing you, I think you might even try that. It would give me great pleasure and joy to watch you do exactly that and many other things that will come from your delightful imagination.

Well, now I know in practical terms just how limitless the Heavenly kingdom is. If I can fly my airplane to the moon, then all sorts of other ideas also come to mind. A good friend of mine passed away, and I know he is in Heaven. I have talked with him several times since his death. He loves motorcycles. I imagine now he could take his motorcycle to the moon as well.

Remember, dear Christian reader, although all these sound nutty and ridiculous, these impractical examples demonstrate how limitless it is in God's Heavenly Kingdom for us, His sacred children. It is indeed a magnificent paradise for all eternity. In my magnificent conversations with our Lord and Savior, Jesus Christ, specifically told me that within the Heavenly kingdom, there are no limitations. If you think about this, now you know why our Heavenly Father demands that not one particle of sin is ever allowed within the gates of the Heavenly kingdom, so stop doing that. Think about it, dear reader.

Also, think about why when some of our holy Father's sacred children choose not to be tested on earth and instead remain within the Heavenly kingdom, there are certain restrictions eternally placed on them. And at the same time, there is no stigma attached to their decision not to come to earth, for it can be said accurately that their love for their Father in Heaven is so great that they do not want to risk anything that might interfere with that love for Him.

Just be faithful dear Christian, and be of good heart, loving our Creator, knowing that in the not-too-distant future, we will be within the Heavenly kingdom living life, an eternal life in paradise. We will have no limitations and the best loving guidance from the Trinity we could ever imagine. It is not all harps and violins. How about football games and baseball too?

6

The Character of Almighty God

This is a wonderful exercise, for we are using our magnificent brain, consciousness, and reasoning power that God has given us to know Him better than we have ever known Him.

One BIG opportunity for learning about God is the character and nature of our Father in Heaven. One God? That idea was preposterous in the minds of people 2000 years ago. So, what are the attributes of our Christian God in Heaven? He is the only true God of all things seen and unseen.

There is no other God but Him. That is the true Biblical view arrived at in the Bible. Abraham first introduced this truth to the Hebrew people long ago, and since then, our understanding of God has expanded greatly. The following is a list of the attributes of our Heavenly Father listed in both the Old and New Testaments.

THE BIBLICAL LIST OF GOD'S ATTRIBUTES OR CHARACTER

To begin with, regarding us, His children are made in His image. He is a loving Father to all believers. Ephesians 1:2; Galatians 1:1; Colossians 1:12; 1 Thessalonians 1:3.

God has emotions to some unknown degree. In the documented dialog in this book, our Father displayed emotions like "I am well pleased." I am sure this cannot be His only emotion. There must be others, like anger and love. He shows us his love for us, His children, in so many different ways, like creating the physical and spiritual realms so we can return to Him. He talks about joy and fulfillment within the Trinity etc. Other indicators are verses in the Bible and the fact that we also have emotions.

Could we have emotions if our Father didn't? Yes, God does have emotions.

God has no beginning or end and is eternal. He always was, He is, and always will be. I know this to be true from personal experience. In one of my discussions with God, I asked Him how He created the physical realm and what He created before our universe. He revealed to me in detail that I will tell you about later in this book. Psalm 90:2; Genesis 1:1; Psalm 102:27

God almighty is always faithful (Immutable) and unchanging in His promises and words. He can be trusted in all things because God himself is truth. Remember what Jesus said, *I am the way, the truth, and the life. No one can go to the Father except through me*. In my time with our Lord, everything, and I mean everything He revealed to me, down to the last detail, was true. Even regarding things about my family that later turned out to be just like He said. Hebrews 13:8; James 1:17; Malachi 3:6; Numbers 23:19; Psalm 102:26-27.

God's justice is perfect and fair. He is no respecter of persons meaning a lowly person in society is treated the same as one in high places. Good deeds will be rewarded, and evil will be punished. One time I misspoke about something that God told me not to say. I forgot, and accidentally I did what I was not supposed to do. Immediately God told me as penance, I had to walk an extra three miles. I remember that until this day— Deuteronomy 32:4; Psalm 19:9; Genesis 18:25.

Love is the very expression of His eternal identity and character. God is perfect love because He always seeks His perfect will in us and desires to see us in the center of His sacred and holy will. He loves us so much that He sent His only begotten son to die and pay for our sins. John 3:16; 1 John 4-8, 16

Omniscience: God knows every detail of our existence. He knows every detail of everything we have ever done, what we are doing to the point that He even knows the number of hairs on our head. He knows our thoughts and what we say. He has perfect recall of all events in the past, no matter how large or small. When God was with me about this book as I was writing it, He already knew its contents from what He told me in a story below. Yes, God does indeed know everything down to the last detail. It is impossible to have any secrets anywhere within God's loving creation, which is explained in multiple places within this book of love.

Omnipotence: God has unlimited power. God is all powerful. There is nothing too hard for Him.

Jeremiah 32:17; 1 Peter 1:5 From what God told me about how He created the spiritual worlds and the two creations, He must be everything the Bible tells us about Him. More on this later.

Omnipresence: God is everywhere. There is no place in Heaven, the spiritual realm, and earth where He is not present. The Psalmist says *no matter where I go, God is there. God is also present in our hearts and minds. Even though many of us who are children of God are very uncomfortable with that thought and will deny the omnipresence of God. There is no place where God isn't.* Psalm 139:7-12; 1 Kings 8:27.

This is a thought that completely torments those followers of Satan, for they desperately want to hide from our Heavenly Father and anybody directly associated with Almighty God. I have personally encountered and lost friends over this very phenomenon. In one case, at my 75th birthday party, I was attacked with lies by the husband of a very good friend of mine of 45 years. The wife defended her husband's lies, so I terminated our long-standing friendship. Nothing is more important than truth, for our Lord and Savior said that He is the way, the truth, and the life, and nobody goes to the Father except by Him. The wife chose very badly.

Righteous: God is sinless, holy, and perfect. All that He does is correct and right and proper. He has no sinful nature and never violates His Word (Scripture). 1 Peter 1:15-16; 1 John 1:5; 1 Samuel 2:2, Deuteronomy 9:14; Psalm 99:9; Deuteronomy 32:4; Psalm 145:17

Sovereign: God is supreme, with no one to answer to. He is completely independent and can make decisions without anyone else's agreement or consent. Isaiah 40:13-14; Deuteronomy 4:39; Ephesians 1

Truth: Everything God says or does is the correct word or action for us to follow. He is ultimately "correct" in every situation. Titus 1:2; Romans 3:4; Romans 11:33; Numbers 23:19)

God knows about everything that is happening in your life. This includes every action and event in your life. There is nothing that God does not know about every one of His children. In a real sense, we are part of God, and He is part of us.

Most people believe that we are here on earth and God is out "there" somewhere in Heaven. This is not the case. There is no spatial difference between God and us, his sacred children. God is omnipresent, meaning that our Almighty Father is right here on earth with us right now. He is so close to every one of His children that we can speak to Him whenever we wish. Remember what Biblical Scripture says about this point. God knows how many hairs you have on your head. Do not be afraid. Read the upcoming story about being with God related to this very book.

HOW TO TALK DIRECTLY TO OUR HEAVENLY FATHER

It is one thing to know God is omnipresent, but it is another thing to understand how to benefit from that. You, as a Christian, may talk to God directly at any time, day or night. It is impossible for God not to hear what you have to say. Nothing is too small for our loving Father. It is impossible for our Father not to be very interested in what you tell Him. God is ALWAYS with us every second of every day. There is NEVER an instant when His loving presence is not intimately close to us.

If something is bothering you, take what you have to say, make the sign of the cross, and say one "Our Father" and one "Hail Mary." Do this in a quiet place with no possible interruptions. Then talk directly to our Father using your normal language. Then after you are done, ask Him to answer you now, not tomorrow or next week, but right now. Ask Him to answer you now immediately after you finish praying. Frame your question or request with a gentle and respectful vocabulary.

Be humble. You are talking to Almighty God, that created everything around you, the whole universe, all that is seen and unseen. He created

YOU! Then prepare yourself to hear His response in many different ways. Good books are written about this very topic. No time here for that now.

On another note, ask God to allow you to feel His presence with you. This is NOT scary stuff, as many would imagine. Doing this gives me a great feeling of security and love that emanates from our Father. Ask Him to be close to you as if you are standing side by side. He will always appear on your right side, never on the left. Remember the sheep and goats story. Open your mind and rest in the image of His being right next to you. I would be very surprised if you did not feel his Divine peaceful presence. I have done this many times, especially when I am feeling down about something. If you do not feel God's loving presence, try again, gently concentrating on relaxing first and slowly saying your two prayers.

You do not have to have a specific issue or problem to talk with our Father. Just say the two prayers above and say to God: "Hi God, I just wanted to greet you and tell you that I love you." God would love it if you did something like this. This is something that I do regularly. I often hear back from our loving Father in Heaven when He says, "I love you." Never be afraid of our loving Father in Heaven, for always remember that He is our personal Creator, and He already resides within us.

His voice is soft, loving, and clear, as I have heard many times. Remember, our Father IS a personal God who is most interested in everything you have to say. Remember, God is on your side. You are created in His image. He wants to hear from you and is never "too busy" to address whatever you have to say. I have done this many times, and He sometimes answers within a second or two. Yup! He is that fast dear friend. Other times God might decide it's better for Him to answer your question later when the time is right. Below is a true story of an incredible event that happened spontaneously one afternoon while writing a different section of this book.

ALMIGHTY GOD IS A VERY PERSONAL GOD

I should note that all communication with the divine is telepathic. If you were standing next to me, you would hear nothing. My dear wife Evangeline experiences this kind of thing with me quite often. Sometimes we will be talking, and suddenly God would break in and tell me something about a topic I had been addressing in my mind. When this happens, my dear wife has no idea what occurred. I then have to tell her something like, "oh, something just occurred to me. I have to write it down. I will be back."

This is just like when the holy golden orb appeared to me on a jet over the Pacific Ocean. When the magnificent, brightly lit golden orb appeared to me, all the other people in the jet saw nothing. That holy appearance changed my life. Details on this mystic experience can be found in a book I wrote several years ago titled ***The Divine Resting On My Shoulder.***

AN UNEXPECTED LOVING ENCOUNTER WITH ALMIGHTY GOD

This next page is a personal story of just one divine incident that happened to me without warning. This event occurred while I was working on a different section of this book. I was in my wife's recliner chair in our meditation room with my laptop computer. It was dark in this room with a few statuettes of the Crucifix, St. Joseph, and our Blessed Virgin Mary. I was not writing at that moment.

Rather, what was on my mind was some of the topics I was going to write about in the book you are reading now. While my thoughts were elsewhere, our Heavenly Father started communicating with me without advance notice or warning. Yes, He does these things according to His timing, not mine.

It is so comforting and wonderful that our Heavenly Father breaks into the flow of my life when He feels He wants to. I openly and lovingly welcome these instances, and in many ways, it's like a sigh of relief for me because it reassures me that my Father in Heaven is with me every moment of my existence.

I again noticed his voice was one of a very loving and kind Father who was gently talking to one of his children. His voice was one of kindness and love. He tends to speak a little slowly. I like that, as I can understand every word He says. I felt very comforted in hearing from Him again.

May 28, 2022
This Is What Our Loving Almighty Father Revealed To Me

What you have said so far in your book I am very pleased. Of what you have written so far regarding the creation of all that you can understand I am also pleased. Ask my son more details on all of that. Tell my children that I love them more than they can possibly imagine. To reassure them tell them I am always with them as they imagine but also in other ways that they cannot.

You are the first that I am allowing to speak with me directly and let that be written. You are a unique child of mine and I am very pleased. Remind my children that I am with them in every way from all the universe to the entire earth that I have crafted so my children could live in the physical and meet me there to learn about me and come closer to me which gives Me great delight.

To create the earth and all before it that made it possible, it did not take what your scientists say in time. For me it was what you would call a blink in time. For you are correct that I live in so many dimensions that you cannot understand. I live within each of your bodies and every cell within. It is I that powers everything within your bodies to let you live within my loving graces for I do love you so very much. Yes, I am in every cell of your bodies and yes, I do know the number of hairs on your head.

You will have a great sense of pleasure and joy once you finish your book. I love you very much my dear son and I want you to know that I am with you in every way for all eternity.

Yes, you are right that I created all my children at the same time and before I created the spiritual realm. Each of you are far different than you know and each of you know and inwardly that I am your Father. Ask my son more details of what I did and what we created before we created the spiritual realm. And ask Him how all the realms relate to each other. I know this is what you want to hear.

I will speak with you again when I want. Always be ready to hear from me for I know you better than you know yourself and I know the questions that were coming to your mind. You have lived your life well and chose to put other people ahead of yourself. This is why I gifted you with being able to talk with me direct. This is special and so are you. I love you for all eternity as you will experience. Lastly, do not cast your book before swine and do not lower yourself to those that hate me and you. I will talk to you again.

Our Father's revelation above flowed nicely into a speech file on my computer. After our Father finished the last sentence above, I was utterly speechless. After He finished, I asked our Father if I got everything correct. He indicated that I did. You just read a word-for-word revelation of what our Almighty God revealed to me that day in May.

HARD TO BELIEVE, BUT TRUE

I understand if you have a hard time accepting the above as true. But we must remember that the Bible is full of miracles like this. One example is the virgin birth of our Lord and Savior, Jesus of Nazareth. God can do anything that He chooses with anybody at any time.

I include this story because it demonstrates just what I talked about regarding God's personal character. Think about it, dear child. We are lucky to be children of such a loving Father in Heaven. Also, remember that our lord and savior, Jesus Christ showed His immense love for us by being born on earth as we are and then voluntarily died on the cross to vanquish our sins. Now we need to love Almighty God in return and follow His rules for us as we live our lives.

I cannot forget the Holy Spirit also. He is always present and guides us as well. Additionally, He urges us to pray and always nudges us to keep a good Christian life. Blessed Mother Mary is such a loving woman who expresses her great love for me differently. Speaking of our Blessed Mother Mary, next is a story about her and me on the freeway.

OUR BLESSED MOTHER MARY ALWAYS IS WATCHING OVER ME

Even on the freeway, she is protecting me even from myself. This is an embarrassing story about when I was driving my 500-hp Corvette. It was a bad traffic situation where I found myself in where a bunch of cars that were close together, constantly getting in each other's way and making aggressive lane changes. I needed to get out of there, so I had to "punch it "to get away from them. In a few seconds, I was going more than 100 mph to get away from some of the crazy drivers now far behind me. I escaped to an opening in the traffic far ahead. Now I was safe. As I was accelerating, I heard our blessed mother Mary say to me, "my son! SLOW DOWN! SLOW DOWN! SLOW DOWN!

After I got back home, I thought about what had happened. I then realized that I was driving down the freeway in my car, taking evasive action using the monster power that my Corvette has to escape from crazy drivers. Then there I was, getting scolded by Mother Mary in Heaven. *Talk* about connections. WOW! Think about this dear Christian friend, Mother Mary was with me all the time and could hold back no longer her concern for me and how fast I went. She works to protect us, even from ourselves.

I realized that our blessed mother Mary was not in a position to perceive why I did what I did to protect myself from the idiots that were driving recklessly so close to me. One of the advantages of driving such a powerful sports car was its evasive capabilities to get away from other reckless drivers so close to me and accelerate into an open spot in traffic where they could not get to me.

Perhaps this story gives a stronger hint to you just how much we are truly loved by the Trinity and, of course, our Blessed Mother Mary. Cherish this story, dear Christian, for it is entirely true. Our blessed mother Mary is always watching over us in this concern with love in her heart every moment of every day. Remember this story always, dear Christian. This is true even in a very powerful Corvette sports car.

7

What Existed Before Creation

Question From Me: Dear God, what actually existed before you created what we know of? What was it like where you existed?

Answer Revealed From Almighty God:

Paradise perfect in every way beyond anything you can possibly understand. Yes, the three of us your Almighty Father me, my begotten son, and the Holy Spirit which connects us all proceeds from us to the dimensions we are contemplating to create.

We love our existence so very much that we wish to expand to include our children, which we want them to love us from their hearts chosen by their free will.

We have free will to do what pleases us and we want our children to inherit this as well. The space and dimensions that we live or exist in are endless. There are no limitations. Everything is absolute perfection. [1]

As you described, we live in a timeless way even when it is so easy to create a timeline that if we wish and begin and end at any particular point. If we wanted, we could create a timeline that you exist in and we then could observe how things develop and proceed to their ultimate fruition. We have done this many times before.

If we want something all we need to do is think it into existence. [2] *Then we can do with it whatever we choose. Each of us three are infinite*

---

[1] Our Father in Heaven created us so as to expand His pleasure and fulfillment by loving His children and they love Him in return through their free will.
[2] Nothing is impossible for Almighty God

beings and complex beyond any kind of your understanding. It gives us great pleasure and joy to interact with each other as we can explore each other in such intimate and joyful ways to see all the different and experience all the different endless facets of our personalities and character. Our interaction and exploration of each other can be endless if we choose. What joy, fulfillment, happiness, and ecstasy we experience by doing this together. We have no need of anything else but the Trinity. [3]

At some timeless point we collectively decided that we wanted to create an additional source of pleasure and enjoyment and love for all three of us. We thought into existence the idea of our children, our sacred children who we love so dearly as we love each other. We bestowed upon our children limited talents but enough for them, you, to thrive in the physical realm we have not yet created. We know you will need this because we already know that one of our future angels will rebel and then hate our children trying his best to destroy what we lovingly created. Our children are part of us.

This is why there is so much evil in your physical world. This is why we created the physical world because we must go into it, the law of degradation are what your scientists call entropy. Nothing in this world including your physical bodies that we thought into existence will be able to exist forever as we do. There will come a point when all those with free will that we bestowed upon all of our children will become a fork in the path where some of you will choose to love your Father, his begotten son me, and the Holy Spirit that binds everything together in glorious love and ecstasy.

We already know of so very much each of you that have chosen to be with your Creator in the perfect paradise We have already created. The others that have rejected us we are so sorrowful about what they will go the way of entropy and dissolve ultimately into nothingness. This is the only kind of pain we have in our hearts but the rebellion of Lucifer with his pride is what created all of this pain and suffering. He will go the

---

[3] Each being of the Trinity that is Almighty God is infinitely complex and joyful for the other two to explore and enjoy.

way of entropy and ultimately on your timeline that we have given you dissolve into nothingness from whence He came. [4]

On your time to mention it is getting short and our begotten son will return to the physical realm and separate those destined for an existence of perfect ecstasy from those who will ultimately dissolve as your universe will. I cannot express to your limited senses just how much we three love you with all of our hearts. That is such a limited way of saying what we really feel for each of you our children that chose to be with us into eternity which will never end. We love you so very much my son we look forward to greeting you and your permanent home with all those that you love and yes, my son including your doggies that you love so much. [5] *I hope this answers your question about our existence before we started to create different realms to make your existence possible with us in timeless paradise.* [6] *I love you.*

Note: Some of the above sentences are not grammatically correct. Some of the thoughts are a little discontinuous and need some intelligent interpretation. I left it that way because it was the way I heard it when Jesus Christ spoke to me. I will never change or interpret anything our Lord and Savior tells me.

Never in my life had I heard such powerful words spoken to me. Our Almighty Father did indeed answer all my questions about the existence of the Trinity before they started to create realms that would be needed to save us, his children, from sin. He explained precisely why they created the different realms I will describe in the following pages.

God so loved his sacred children so much that not only did He send his only begotten son, but He also created multiple realms that would be needed for our salvation on an individual basis. Yes, God loves us so much that He created us in his image and created this universe we live in

---

[4] Astronomers, astrophysicists, and cosmologists are concluding that our universe due to dark energy will expand without end and result in nothingness. This is a mainstream hypothesis.
[5] God knows and understands each of us in magnificent detail. He even knows about my love for my dogs.
[6] God loves us so very much that if He did not create the spiritual realm and importantly the physical realm, we would not be able to be redeemed from sin and not be able to join the Trinity in their timeless realm of infinite joy and fulfillment. More on this later.

so we can decide through our belief in Him and loving actions to join Him in an eternal loving paradise. He also created other realms designed to support our lives on this physical earth to make it possible for us to choose our Almighty Father so we can live with Him in paradise for eternity.

So, dear reader, remember this. The entire universe that we live in, all the stars, and everything else contained within it has been specifically designed and fine-tuned for us and only us to receive redemption from sin if we choose through our own free will. It is for this reason that the entire universe exists. Think of that, dear reader, and think about how precious you are to Almighty God if He would do all of this for your redemption.

8

The Decision to Create Sacred Children

There was NO beginning. There was only Almighty God. There was the Father, the only begotten Son, and the Holy Spirit which proceeds from them to the dimensions they have already created. The dimensions of the realms that the Trinity lives in are endless and has no limitations. Everything is absolute perfection.

Question to God: I know that all your sacred children are like everything else created by yourself and you unlimited love and power. When was it dear Lord that the Holy Trinity decided to create us, all of your children and why did you decide to do this?

I was sitting on my lounge chair with my computer in my lap. I had speech to text software running. I could speak into the microphone the thoughts that came to me from the Almighty. Dear reader you probably never thought of things like this but in your life except the written text from the Bible but I do wonder when God decided to create us sacred children out of nothingness. This text is meant to enrich your understanding of the great love and care our Father in Heaven has for you and me. After all, each one of us is unique from all the rest are but still made in the image of our Heavenly Father.

CREATING GOD'S SACRED CHILDREN/ A PERSONAL DISCUSSION

Dear Lord God, am I speaking with you now?

"Yes, my beloved son you most certainly are. I love you ever so much. You are very special in the eyes of us gives me great joy and delight to tell you these things of us. Your interest in the Trinity gives us delight

and joy and when your book is done you too will receive joyous delight through what you have written. Your question is about for now how you and the rest of God's children were created. I will answer that.

This was eons ago, I paused for a moment for your mind to catch up with me, are you ready now?

I think so. (Me)

Previously the Trinity had decided that we wanted children that would reflect our beauty and some of the characteristics that we have between us. We wanted our children to have free will as we do. We wanted them to have a limited number of the powers that we have so as to prepare them for one day they would join us in the dimensions that we occupy and they would be able then to experience some of the joys and some of the ecstasy that we experience and enjoy within our lives.

They will be able to experience this with us. It is beyond your understanding what we are able to do, what we are able to experience and the pure ecstasy and depth of love that we are able to experience by being who we are. But we have given you as our children the capability to reach magnificent heights that US, our children are able to reach if you develop the capabilities, we have already given you.

The experiential part of being us is something that you cannot understand. And for now, you cannot understand the experiential part of what you can become but you can achieve a wonderfully delicious and magnificent joyful existence that a few of your religious traditions have only hinted at.

My dear son Richard is bringing you this message at my will so you can understand us more deeply also very much, the Trinity today loves you so very much, so very deeply as we extend our arms to every one of you and love, complete love, and acceptance. We pray that you, every one of you accept our offer of peace and acceptance to pray on your knees and accept us as your God of peace and love so that there will never again be one act of violence or selfishness in any way from this moment on.

Resist any person that advocates in any way any act of hatred, selfishness, or division for surely, they will lead you to hell and ultimately you will be dissolved into nothingness. Richard is my messenger to you. Listen to him well for he will lead you to me. I will go now. There will be further messages in this book from God your Father in his name I love you. Amen."

A few months later I asked a highly related question about where we as God's children were thinking that we were in the Heavenly Kingdom with the Trinity. We were spiritual beings at the time. Yes, both you and I were spiritual beings inside the Heavenly Kingdom with the Trinity for eons of time before we elected to come to earth to make our eternal decision.

Answer From Almighty God:

"Paradise perfect in every way beyond anything you can possibly understand.

"At some timeless point we collectively decided that we wanted to create an additional source of pleasure and enjoyment and love for all three of us. We thought into existence the idea of our children, our sacred children who we love so dearly as we love each other.

Please pause for more than a moment. This is one of the most important parts of this book. It points out just how important each child of the Trinity really is. We are infinitely loved by all three members of the Trinity for all eternity, just as they loved each other. We all need to deeply think about this. Each of us need to put Almighty God at the center of our lives as we go about doing what we need to do on this earth. If you choose not to and consciously reject God, then you will be with Satan and all his demons as the physical realm will dissolve into nothingness due to the law of entropy which is already in place and working right now. It is the physical law that takes order into disorder, randomness, or chaos.

We bestowed upon our children, you, limited talents but enough for them to thrive in the physical realm we have not yet created. We know you will need this because we already know that one of our future angels will rebel and then hate our children trying his best to destroy what we lovingly created. Our children are part of us.

We love our existence so very much that we wish to expand to include our children, which we want to them to love us from their hearts and chosen by their free will. We have free will to do what pleases us and we want our children to inherit this as well.

How can I possibly describe the above magnificent words above revealed by Almighty God. It describes why we exist as God's sacred children and why we have the different talents we do including the magnificent gift of free will that all of us possess. The above sentences also describe as I have stated multiple times in this book why all creation that is seen and unseen exists. It is from the infinite love that Almighty God has for us so that we, his sacred children, have the opportunity to choose to live with the Trinity in the Paradise that we cannot imagine, for all eternity. If you learn nothing else from this extensive book, learn what the previous thoughts tell you.

THE COMING ETERNAL CHOICE FOR EACH OF US

It has been said many times that each of us on earth has a choice to choose between our Heavenly Father or Satan. It also needs to be recognized that we do not fully understand the depths of our own spiritual being. Our Father has given us free will. What we say and do on earth is driven by the deepest parts of our spiritual being and free will. What we create on earth will reflect what lies deep within us. It is also a reflection of our free will, good or bad.

To discover what lies deep within us, we must be tested fairly so that we will know what is at the core of our being. So, almost all of you, God's children, choose to spend a life on earth which will test you to the very bottom of your existence. There will be suffering involved, and there will be attacks by Satan in many different ways while you're on the earth. It is your response to these temptations and attacks that will demonstrate to you what you have decided to make of yourself.

THOSE WHO CHOOSE NOT TO GO TO EARTH

Some of you will not choose to go to earth because you do not want to take the risk of never coming back to the Heavenly Kingdom. This choice is honored by your Father. In these cases, his children will remain within the Heavenly Kingdom. But they will be restricted in what they can do and where they can go. Your Heavenly Father will never permit anything that resembles sin or potential sin within the Heavenly Kingdom. So proper loving measures are taken to accommodate his children that choose not to take the earthly test. All of us in the Heavenly Kingdom completely understand this choice and honor all the children that choose this way.

There is never any embarrassment, or second-class standing in doing this, for all of the Heavenly Kingdom loves these children just as much as all the rest. This decision not to go to earth can be viewed as a beautiful act of deep love for the Trinity. These children that choose this path do not want to risk in any way not being able to come back and live with their Heavenly Father in the Kingdom. This is viewed very positively. The others that choose to go to earth are viewed as wonderfully adventurous and want to show all creation their deepest love for their Heavenly Father and enjoy their eternal existence with the entire Trinity. They said the truth is that many of God's sacred children succumb to the satanic temptations on earth and do not return. All of this decision-making is of everyone's free will. Nothing is forced upon any of our Fathers' children.

The following is a testimony from Almighty God regarding what I have just spoken about. There is some redundancy and run-on sentences, but these are the words of our loving Father when I asked Him about my encounter within the Heavenly realm and seeing my first grandchild preparing for her birth that was coming in a few months. Now she is in college and is a bright student, and I am proud of her.
My question was simply what happens for each spiritual child that comes to earth. What preparations were made while God's children were still in the Heavenly Kingdom before they were born into the earth?

BEFORE WE ARE BORN TO EARTH
September 30, 2022, 9:46 AM
Jesus Christ

It is a lengthy process my dear son. No need for now to go into the selection process of who of God's spiritual children will be the ones next to go to the physical earth. That is a process that is very detailed and arranged to meet the needs and preferences of each child while they are in the Heavenly Kingdom. After the selection process is completed and agreed to that their coming life on the earth will satisfy the spiritual needs of each child. And also, after it is agreed to that their position and location on the earth will be fair.

This means to reveal what their true feelings are, like wanting to come back to the Heavenly realm for all eternity or choose to be with Satan in a completely disordered manner where there is no morality or any other fundamental behavioral standards that are to be met. Those who want that will choose Satan with the understanding that at some point in their future they will, as you point out about entropy, they will slowly dissolve back into nothingness from which they came.

After the selection process is completed to meet the individual needs of the children of God, they will then need to go through a preparation process next. This includes many things such as acclimatizing them for a life in the physical realm. Remember, none of God's children have any idea what that is like for having been spirit beings for their entire existence. They must get used for example to not have what they want instantaneously. They have to understand what hardship and satanic dishonesty are. Because they have never experienced that either.

They will not understand the experience of dishonesty and other features of the disaster Satan has brought to the earthly realm. This is why little children on earth believe everything they are told and are so gullible all the falsity that exists on earth.

It is only after each child feels comfortable enough with what is coming and the consequences that are involved regarding their fundamental decision of yes to God or yes to Satan. It is only then that they will be connected with their guardian angel that will be with them throughout their entire physical existence. They will then come to know the family that they will be born into and they will understand the general dynamics of family life on earth and the specific family they will be born into.

Nothing is left to chance. For this is always the way of your Father. Everything is perfectly planned with no random chances. After this fairly long period of preparation then they will decide at what point of their mother's pregnancy will they inhabit the physical baby developing in their mother's womb. This varies from child to child. During their mother's pregnancy it is accurate to say that a child of God in the womb is a developing human being blessed by the entire Trinity.

This is the general outline of what happens before a child of God is allowed to be born into the earthly realm. We all pray for each child as they leave that they will pass the test of evil and return back to us in the Heavenly realm. This whole process will reveal what their true fundamental free will choice is.

It is only on earth that each child of God will completely understand themselves and why they make whatever choice they do. And lastly, they will decide a major theme of their life. Like you my dear son, you chose your life as putting all other people ahead of yourself.

This is a very hard choice to make for it involves much suffering on the planet Earth. But you chose this my dear son before you were born on the earth. And I am so very proud of you my dear son for you have achieved spiritual greatness that is not recognized by those around you. And now it is very good that you will include in this book the experience you had when you visited your first granddaughter while she was at the last stages of preparation for her birth into the physical earth. I love you.

STORY OF ME SEEING MY FIRST GRANDCHILD BEFORE HER BIRTH

I know this to be true from my personal experience. Approximately 18 years ago, I anxiously anticipated my first grandchild's birth. I was so happy knowing that I would be a grandfather soon. It turned out that it was a girl. I was so anxious to hold her and say to my new grandchild that I loved her. One afternoon I was in my meditation room. As usual, the room was dark, and I had my earplugs in to avoid being distracted. I was sitting in my easy chair and thinking about my soon-to-be grandchild.

All of a sudden, I felt as if I was leaving my body. The next thing I knew, I was in a very quiet room with lots of activity. It was like a quiet hustle and bustle going on. I could hear the noise of spirits shuffling around doing this, that, and the other thing. I am not sure what they were doing.

I could see many small spiritual beings with the appearance of what I just described that God's children take before they are born into this physical world. They all look identical. You cannot tell them apart one from the other. Even though every spirit child is unique, one of a kind. They were all the same size, and they were shuffling around. I was told that the spirits I saw were all preparing for a life on Earth. What that entailed, I did not know.

One interesting note is that even though all these spirit beings looked the same, they were not the same. Remember that each child of God is one of a kind, unique from all the rest. This means that every one of the look-alike white spirit beings I saw had one-of-a-kind potentials, fundamental personalities, interests, capabilities, and talents. All of these differences are to manifest in the baby after birth. These characteristics of each child will grow in maturity over the years of life they have.

One day in prayer, I asked our Father why I have these spiritual gifts when no one else I know has them. He answered, ***it is because of the decision you made before you were born.*** *God, what was that I said? God responded with these exact words,* ***you made the decision that you would put all others before yourself. This is why you are gifted this way.***

THE SHAPE OF BABIES STILL IN THE SPIRITUAL INCUBATOR IN THE KINGDOM

The form that all of them (the pre-born babies) take <u>looks like a semitransparent, very puffy pure white bowling pin</u>. But their upper body is bigger. They have two very small coal-black eyes and a small black nose. There were perhaps a few dozen of these "future baby" spirits moving around. Then suddenly, one of these little spirits came very close to me, perhaps 18 inches or so. This spirit being knew me somehow. Yes, she knew who I was, and she just kept on looking at me. I instantly knew who she was too. This little white spirit was my first granddaughter about three months before she was due to be born to my daughter-in-law. I did not know what to say to her, and she said nothing in return. We just looked at each other, knowing who we were. After a while, it got awkward, and my visit to the spiritual realm nursery ended, and I found myself back in my meditation room in my chair.

I sat in my chair for a while, pondering what had just happened. I could not get over the fact that I was gifted ever so much to have this experience available to me. Without me asking, Almighty God knew what was on my mind and what I wanted to have happened. And consistent with his ways, God silently granted my prayer, and that afternoon I made the trip, the instantaneous trip, to the Heavenly nursery where my first granddaughter was. My dear people, think very much about this kind of event because it is normal in God's creation.

THE FUTURE

Please pause for more than a moment. This is one of the most important parts of this book. It points out just how important each child of the Trinity is. We are infinitely loved by all three members of the Holy Trinity for all eternity, just as they love each other. We all need to think deeply about this. Each of us needs to put Almighty God at the center of our lives as we go about doing what we need to do on this Earth.

If you choose to and consciously reject God, then you will be with Satan, and all his demons, as the physical realm will dissolve into nothingness due to the law of entropy. This process will take all things related to Satan back into the nothingness from which they came. Entropy is already evident and working right now throughout our universe regarding all things physical. Remember, entropy is a property of the universe that increases the randomness and chaos of physical matter. The physical law takes order into disorder, randomness, chaos, and ultimate nothingness. This will happen to all God's children who reject their Heavenly Father. Jesus Christ himself said beware of the second death. This is what He was talking about.

Ever wonder why we age as time goes on? Aging is a given regarding our lives on Earth. No one bothers to question it or wonder why it exists. Aging is because our bodies, our physical bodies, are giving way to the force of entropy, increasing the randomness of all the matter within our bodies. If somebody complains to you that they are aging, tell them they are only suffering from the effects of entropy. Jesus refers to the current scientific term entropy as "the law of degradation" No matter where you look on this earth, this law is in full force and effect. The appearance of age in people, of rust, of mechanical machines wearing out are all sublet to entropy or the law of degradation.

They will have no idea what you're talking about, yet you will be 100% correct. The above text from our Heavenly Father reveals their motivations for creating you and me. God sounds very much like a loving Father here on Earth, frankly. He wants his sacred children to enjoy all the good things He experiences. And wants us to inherit a lot of it too. He wants us to have eternal life full of great enjoyment, love, and fulfillment. We will not have limitations in Heaven as we do here on Earth. We will have total freedom to come and go as we please.

Look what He did to give us a way out of the mess Satan caused (hate, destruction, chaos, confusion, and all the other rotten things) in our world today. Satan has also attracted many of God's children to do his bidding on Earth, people that put themselves and their selfish goals above all others of God's children, the source of all deceit and lies we have to put up with while on this planet. Just think about what it will be like living in a gorgeous place where there is no sin. remember, when one person puts himself above the needs of others of God's sacred children, it can be said that this one person is worshiping himself above all others of God's children that are made in the image of God. This is very much like the sin of blasphemy. This is precisely what the Pharisees did when they said that the miracle Jesus Christ performed with the deaf and blind man, that Jesus used the power of Beezelbub. In essence, the Pharisees attacked God himself.

Unlike Earth, which is polluted with sin and all that comes from it. After all, we are physically born onto this planet Earth, and we naturally understand that conflict derived from sin is a natural part of life. Only a few of us search for the underlying reasons why that is. Many of the reasons for all the conflict on Earth has been explained in this book. One day sin will be dissolved back into the nothingness from the force of God that we call entropy. But this will not happen for a long time. That will be until we return to the Heavenly Kingdom to enjoy eternity with our Savior Jesus Christ, our Heavenly Father, and the Holy Spirit.

9

Designing God's Sacred Children

The following text is exactly what God Almighty revealed to me. There are a few spots where some sentences have extra words that do not make sense, but I included them for completeness.

One thing we need to be sensitive to is time. Here in the real physical world, our time proceeds at a much different pace than it does in the Heavenly Kingdom.

So, depending on the desire of Almighty God, a day could seem like a thousand years here on earth. It is undetermined how long it took the Trinity to design our human bodies. Yet Almighty God does say, "it took us a very long time." It is exceedingly interesting that our Godly-designed bodies have been uniquely designed to be interfaced with BOTH the physical realm and the spiritual realm equally well with ease.

This is necessary to carry out our mission of deciding which road to take while we are on this earth for all eternity. Our choice is extremely clear for us, dear children of God. Either the Heavenly road with Almighty God or the Satanic road to hell and obliteration into nothingness. God created/thought us, his children, into existence before the spiritual and physical realms were created. We all dwelled with the Trinity in The Heavenly Kingdom with God our Father for a delightfully long period of time. Where else would we be when you think about it? Of course, we all wanted to be with our parents that loved us more that can be described.

July 10, 2022, 9:46 AM
Jesus Christ

It took us a very long time to design the features and characteristics of our sacred children. We knew they would be crafted in our image. What does that mean? It means that they would have some of the capabilities that we have. It does not mean that they would look like us because we are formless and are something that has no boundaries that you can define. Yet for our children you would need to have boundaries because for us to interface with you, you would need to live in the physical world that we have not created yet.

We would need to create a physical world that you would live in but also interface with a spiritual realm where we could communicate with you. So, we would have to create a being that was physical in nature and could survive in a physical realm that could also thrive in a physical environment. But this being should also be able to communicate with us his Creator or so that we can give him the opportunity to choose whether or not he wanted to through his free will join us in the Heavenly realm or choose the sinful realm after the coming rebellion by Lucifer.

We already know that Lucifer will rebel against us and through his hatred he will attack our children and tempt all of our children to follow him. We know that most of our children will be fooled and follow him into hell where ultimately, they will be dissolved into nothingness. They will go the way of entropy run wild in the physical realm. Those who choose through their free will and love for us, they will join us in an unimaginably beautiful and loving paradise that they will live with us forever eternally with no end.

We needed to design a physical body that had two fundamental characteristics primarily one that could withstand the biological requirements to remain healthy for a relatively long period of time such that they could grow and prosper with sufficient time, since there will be time, the dimension of time, to learn about our existence and decide whether they want to follow us through their free will and love us, accept us, or not and demonstrate that in this physical realm and that will be recorded throughout all history.

Or if they reject our offer of love and decide to follow Satan instead in which case, they will choose the path of obliteration and ultimately dissolve into nothingness. They will be using their free will to choose this. Their bodies must also be able to reproduce so as to bring on new generations until our Almighty Father chooses to bring me back in My second coming.

This brings on a whole host of biological challenges for us in this is what takes us the most amount of time, to design we chose the path, actually the only path, of something you call DNA and RNA. It is extremely complex and your scientists have come a long way in understanding its intimate complexity. Some of your scientists have foolishly said that what we have designed occurred accidentally. We still laugh about that. Some of your scientists have observed that the whole universe of yours was designed by us so carefully that it was indeed designed to in some cases one part in 10 to the 140th power of fine design so that the earth could support human life. [7]

They are correct. Now back to designing life, we had to design the human body so that it could fend for itself in the features of a planet that could sustain itself for billions of years and we did so, with the planet you call earth. There is no other planet in your universe that is in a place of your universe quite like the one where you are at now.

There will come a time not too long from now where it will not be possible for earth to support life any longer. Look around you to your sister planets even they cannot support life on the earth there are reasons for that. [8] *The first human beings that we set up on the earth had a full complement of chromosomes and was able to reproduce with a female that we also put on the earth, your story of Adam and Eve is close to the truth. They did not come out of the swamp as the fairytale that the Abiogenesis people like to promote. It happened at our will. We*

---

[7] Dear Dr. Hugh Ross: I dedicate this section to all your hard work proving how God created the universe

[8] Scientists in the field of astrophysics, astronomy and cosmology in the last 20 years have come to understand that the earth has enjoyed a Goldilocks cycle that has supported life for the last billion years or so. But that cycle is coming to an end very shortly. It will become quickly harder and harder to support life on our planet as it does today. Dr. Hugh Ross and others have published books on this topic like The Improbable Planet

lovingly put them there that a most beautiful place surrounded by much food on delicious trees and a stream to support human life and then we woke them up male and female.

And things proceeded from there. It did take us what you would call a long time to design the cyclical helix that is self-reproducible within the cells of the human body but yes, we did design that through our thoughts, it was a collective effort of the Trinity. It is a beautiful work of art and we are proud of what we did for our children our sacred to us and we plan to have every child of ours be full members of the Kingdom. All they have to do is say yes to our offer of love and then they will be members of the Holy Kingdom with paradise forever eternal.

Our plan was very simple. The male and the female after we woke them became the stewards of the garden which was full of delicious food of many different kinds that would completely nourish the needs of the male and female and all their children. This is the Adam and Eve that is in your Bible. We also knew that at some point Lucifer would appear to them and tempt them away from our sacred plan where they would multiply upon the earth and grow and become fruitful in and of themselves and fill the land with their descendants many times over. They would never feel pain or destruction. For they were our children. Such things as pain would remain unknown to them. Pain is something that is unknown to the children of God.

However, Lucifer had grown in his hatred of Almighty God to the point where he could not stand himself any longer and he became consumed with his hatred of God's children who were made in his image and became so obsessed with destroying God's pure and perfect children on earth. As you know, God gave all his children the gift of free will. This is because before we created our children, we wanted each of them to love for us voluntarily and choose us freely of their free will to love us freely and not be forced in any. This is the only way it can be otherwise, what good is the love of a robot.

Lucifer took on a form of a beautiful animal that lived in the trees. It could speak beautifully, and its breath was succulent and soft. It was beguiling to behold. It lived in many different trees. But there was one tree that both male and female was told that they should never eat of its fruit, it was the tree of the knowledge of good and evil.

For eating of that tree would give the male and female the knowledge that they should never know. It would wipe away their pure innocence and they would be pure no more. They would become a tainted creature that could now know the manner of sinful ways and could never return to their purity of Almighty God.

From that moment God not only would the male and female be impure, but their impurity would be transmitted by the seed of the male throughout all the generations to follow and it would never stop. It would now take an act of blood sacrifice of God himself to redeem what Satan has brought to God's children. That would not come until many generations have come and gone. Lastly pain and suffering has entered the world and stay there with mankind until the end of time.

10

A Poetic View for Both of God's Creations

Both creation and redemption are intimately linked. The reason for creation is to allow redemption for God's sacred Children. Both are finely tuned to the tight specifications of the human body, both physical and biological. Additionally, astrological creation is finely tuned to the hyper specifications of the earth to support human life for long periods of time. Also, the cosmos is finely tuned to support the Milky Way galaxy to support our earth for long periods of time to support it for human life for long periods of time. Break one link in that chain, and no human life, ever! Evolutionists are full of crap! Truth be told, God did everything! Our story begins:

God's Sacred Children

Within eons of timeless time the Holy Trinity decided with excitement
It was something that would bring them great pleasure and enjoyment.
They would create sacred children that would bring them great joy.
These sacred children would be created in their holy image.
The Trinity is all knowing, knows what's to come with great visage.
So, they will be given needed gifts of specially important, free will.

They would create sacred children in their own image with great gifts.
These gifts would be such that would carry them through.
Two realms created by our loving father in the blink of an eye.
These two realms fit the sacred children perfectly.
The physical to procreate the generations to come in harmony.
The spiritual to speak with our Heavenly Father even if imperfectly.

God is the essence of all that is true, all that is good, all that is love.
Fly into our hearts dear Lord, like a white and pure beautiful dove.
The Trinity all together, three yet one,

Your Life's Purpose in God's Grand Design

To save us from sin, he sent us His only begotten son.
Total fulfillment, time before time, bedrock of all foundations.
God cornerstone of all that is truth, complete with deep adoration.

Within all that was, all that would come children made in their image.
They would create to their perfection for all the ages.
And so it was, again in the blink of an eye our loving Father.
Created all of us His Sacred Children within the Heavenly Kingdom
Our loving Father is not a cookie cutter, all of us are completely unique.
We played with our loving Father for unknown eons of timeless time,
Each of us played, learned with our Father separately and loving Him,

Loving Him so deep as a child can so pure, innocent, with our whims.
Our loving Father spent individual time with each of us herein.
Satan rebelled, Adam and Eve original sin all generations forward.
Yes, all sacred children sin our spirits would have a sinful blot.
Then sometime later we knew it was to earth we all could choose or not.
Most of us chose earth, test our love of Father, most weak we got.

Made in His image and ever so pure. We came to life Adam and Eve
From the stars through space God certainly lives, He loves us all.
Coming together His divine nurturing we desperately need.
But if without it we will wither away, yes indeed!
The words of God to us guidance so infinite and precise,
Look at the Mandelbrot, only perfection could ever suffice.

God knew His sacred children's salvation before Adam's fall.
So, we will prepare creation, not one but two, realms also to be.
The first for my children to speak with me, love close to Me.
Free will to choose Almighty Father, to choose now for all eternity.
The second, procreate sacred children, live within God's morality.
Live by the sacred 10, boot out satan in his forsaken ass.
He is clever and wily and sneaks through the cracks.

Let him in, sooner or later, will break your Christian working back.
The spiritual realm for God's children: to talk with their Father.
The physical realm to procreate so more sacred children may come.
Bring many of God's children to populate the earth, the test is here!
Learn all you can about who and what you are. Pass the test dear child!

Your Life's Purpose in God's Grand Design

Treat others and love others as you love yourself, the kingdom awaits. Treat others badly, lie and cheat, murder and scorn, results in hate, wailing and shrieking, hell, and then disassembly into nothingness from whence you came there will you return to your fate.

God Creates His Children In The Spirit

My dear fellow Christian, with great joy, I have the immense honor from our Heavenly Father to bring to you the Trinity's deepest thoughts about all creation and their sacred children. This next section discusses the creation of us as spiritual, sacred children of our loving Father in Heaven. There are a number of things attached to this topic that I know you will find revealing and sometimes humorous due to my observations of what I see in the Heavenly realm.

Yes, my son God did first create all his children in the blink of an eye. From your time perspective it took quite a while but from our time perspective it was indeed a blink of an eye. Remember your Heavenly Father lives in so very many different dimensions all at the same time. He created all his children in spiritual form first. Each one of them was completely different in mind and in spiritual body. Each one had different talents different aspirations different everything.

They all look the same if you were to gaze upon them from the outside. Previously you said they looked like white bowling pins and yes laughably you are right. And their eyes did indeed look like small black dots with the nose stuck in the middle. I laughed the first time I heard you say that because that's precisely what they look like. My dear son you do have a wonderful sense of humor. That is one of the things I certainly love about you.

Our Heavenly Father wanted to enjoy their existence for a very long period of time in the Heavenly Kingdom before He provided them a physical body so they would be able to choose whether or not they would stay with Him in the Heavenly Kingdom because He did indeed give them all free will as the three of us have free will. This is very important because God has his infinite love and free will and will never force anything upon anyone under any circumstance which includes all of his beloved children. I will rest for now because I've gotten way ahead of you.

(This was always a problem for me when receiving sacred thoughts from either our Almighty Father, our Lord and Savior Jesus Christ, and to a lesser degree, our beloved and blessed Mother Mary. To them, I must feel like a glacier moving at 8 cm per year trying to keep up with their thoughts which I know are a zillion times faster than mine. Who knows, perhaps Almighty God creates more universes while I am going from one word to the next. This is a good example of being in multiple timelines.)

Again, as a reminder, your Father in Heaven knew from the very beginning that one of his angels, Lucifer, would rebel against Him and would attack all of his beloved children and would succeed to a very large degree and turning most of his children against Him in the physical world. This would be a very heart wrenching and heartbreaking experience for your loving Father in Heaven. But your beloved Father felt it was worth it because the remaining children would be choosing your Father to love Him for all eternity through their free will and they would adore Him completely through their love in their hearts and that would give all three of us such enormous joy that it is something we have never experienced before and it is something that we look forward to with heartfelt thanks.

So. all of God's children spent a wonderful enormous and uncountable amount of time with the three of us in the Heavenly Kingdom before they started to be born into both the spiritual and physical realms which your Heavenly Father did co-create simultaneously. The spiritual realm and the physical realm depend upon each other just as the physical bodies of his children do. One relies upon the other just as the brains of his children are split into two pieces where one amplifies the spirit and one amplifies the physical. In this manner your loving Almighty Father is ever so close to each one of his children that He loves so very much.

Question: What was life like for God's children in the Heavenly Kingdom before they were born to earth?

During this time when God's children were all spiritual beings there were no limits, they could think of something and to some degree it would appear before their very tiny black eyes and behold there it was, they would play with things that they created and they would enjoy each other immensely and they would cooperate with each other and they would love each other enormously the cooperation between each other was a joy to behold. There was no male and there was no female.

For that, they would have to wait until they were born into the physical world. Oh, they had such a wonderful time they could go from here to there just by thinking about it. They really had no limits. There were oceans. There were mountains there were deserts. There was anything you could possibly imagine, and it was impossible for them to get hurt. They could play hide and seek as you could imagine, and they invented different games as children do. Their loving Father took all of this in with great joy and happiness and He delighted in absolutely everything that He saw. And so did the other two of us as well. The wonderment of children is so contagious, and the joy abounded beyond anything we imagined.

For a fleeting moment we in the Trinity thought perhaps we could let things stay as they were but we knew we couldn't keep our children in a bottle for we had given them free will and an imagination as well. So, sooner or later within any kind of dimension of time we knew that they would become restless and that is something we cannot bring upon our beautiful children.

So, it was then that your Almighty Father in Heaven created both the spiritual realm and the physical realm together. They are intended to work together because as you have said before our children's physical body is made of two parts, a physical part and a spiritual part. More on this in detail later. My dearest son Richard, I love you so very much I want to thank you for writing this book so my words can be spread to many others of my children. Your blessings will be great.

Amen.

12

The Very Core of God's Magnificent Sacred Children

Question: Dear Lord, I know all of us children of God, were created as spiritual beings. You said earlier that we spent numerous eons of time in the Heavenly Kingdom with our Father, with you and the Holy Spirit. This time was filled with joy, fulfillment, and learning about ourselves and creation. Lucifer's rebellion happened long before our creation. The Trinity working together, created all that is seen and unseen for us children to have a pathway back to the Heavenly Kingdom.

My question is based on this: were we (God's sacred children) compelled to be born on this earth for our redemption after the fall of Adam and Eve? Were we given a choice by our Father to stay in the Kingdom?

July 30, 2022, 10:46 AM
Jesus Christ

My dearest son, you have asked a marvelous question. As you know after you were created you were given the same gift of free will that your Father also bestowed upon all his angels and the love between all of the individuals that are part of all of God's creation. This also applies, my dear son, to creations that are beyond the ones that you know of. There are more.

The situation before earth was habitable in its galactic development was that you and all of God's sacred children were such a loving and completely endearing part of the Heavenly Kingdom. All of you were completely sinless. I have to emphasize that all of you were actually incapable of any sort of sin even though you possessed the wonderful gift of free will. However, when Satan rebelled against your Heavenly Father everything changed. This event caused the potential for God's sacred children to also fall away from us in the Holy Trinity. This rebellion happened long before your Father created all of you along with Adam and Eve and so on.*

Dear Lord: When was Lucifer's rebellion? Was it before or after God created all his sacred children?

Think this through dear son. your Father knew long before we decided to create children in His image that Lucifer, one of his powerful angels, would rebel against Him in a horrifically sinful manner. Under no circumstances would God allow his sacred children to be exposed to Lucifer's evil while you were in the Heavenly Kingdom. Therefore, before you were lovingly created in your Father's image, Lucifer and his followers were cast out of the Heavenly Kingdom. Also, he was cast out long before the earth had developed to the point where it would support human life.

POTENTIAL SACRED CHILDREN SIN

So, at some point in the vast history of your sacred existence, simultaneously the conditions were that you were not created yet, Lucifer and his rebel angels had been cast out of the Heavenly realm down to the pre-existing spiritual realm, the part called hell made special for Satan and his demons, and to the earth where Lucifer now called Satan was forced to dwell with his angels now called demons. It was only after this that all of us in the Trinity engaged in the glorious and loving creation of each one, each special and unique one of God's sacred children. You were then great citizens of the Heavenly realm where there was no conflict, where there was no Lucifer or rebellious angels.

There was no sin in the air so to speak that would tempt any of God's children. This is why everyone of you was completely sinless and was unable to succumb to temptation of any kind. All of that potential sin was previously cast out of the Heavenly Kingdom when Lucifer and his angels were gone.

Now after that, because of Lucifer's pride that bubbled up from deep inside him, it became unavoidable that you in some manner in infinite time would be exposed to sin within the multiple creations of Almighty God.

You may ask how could an angel created in perfection could have such a negative emotion deep inside them? I will not go into all the details but I will tell you that it has to do with balance of all creations and symmetry of everything in its totality. Remember, all God's children have no knowledge of everything else that occurs in created form from your Heavenly Father. There is the other that exists as well. That is all I want to tell you at this time.

All of this is a background to answer your first question, you were given a choice to come to the earth so as to be tested by your free will to choose your eternal destiny. Choose God for eternal paradise living with the Trinity in the Heavenly Kingdom and voluntarily obey the rules set forth for his children. Or choose to succumb to Satan's lure of false freedom and slowly dissolve back into nothingness from where everything associated with Satan will go.

Were all of God's children given a free choice whether to be born on the earth? Yes! God will never force himself upon anything within all his creations. All have a choice. You, my dearest son made your choice to live on the earth for a blink in time to resolve your eternal destiny. As I told you before my dearest one, before you were born you chose to live a life where you will always put others, ahead of yourself. This is a remarkable choice while you were still within the Heavenly Kingdom. You wanted to emulate what is the essence of the Trinity. And so, you have lived such a life and you are yet to know and feel the glorious amount of love that is waiting for you when you return. You have suffered so much in the name of your Almighty Father.

All of these choices are also available to every one of your Father's unique children. As it turns out almost all of God's spiritual children chose to live a life on earth. They wanted to be tested about their love for their Father and his ways. In this manner everything that is deeply inside each child will be exposed for all to see including themselves. Many times, even God's sacred children do not know or are aware of what lurks at the core of their free will being.

In a sense you could call this a purification process for the benefit of all God's children and the physical and spiritual realms. All of God's sacred children did know that if they had fatal free will flaws deep inside them, living within the Heavenly Kingdom would be torturous for them. This is because living a Holy life would seem like prison to them sooner or later. They would rather know now by going to earth and finding out what boils inside them.

Free will is an overwhelmingly powerful gift to give to anyone. God did not want to create drones or robots. All of us in the Trinity wanted those children that love us by their own choice of free will. What pleasure be derived out of being loved only because they were told to. That kind of love is an imposter and not love at all. This would fly into the face of the true character of the three of us in the Trinity. For as I said while I was on earth, I am the way, the truth, and the life. It is truth that makes everything work in such a loving manner. Without that nothing is worth anything at all. It is the truth of each child's freedom will that guides their destiny one way or the other.

Now, what about the few of God sacred children that were afraid to look inside themselves and go to earth to find out? Consistent with our deep love for all our children, they may stay inside the Heavenly Kingdom for all eternity. However, they will live freely in a restricted part of the Kingdom. Their lives will be utterly glorious, filled with the love of us in the Trinity, the love of the angels that surround them and serve them, the love of all the other children who preferred to stay in the Kingdom and not sojourn to earth.

Their existence will indeed be joyous and wonderful for all eternity. But they will do so in a much smaller and restricted part of the Heavenly Kingdom. All of us love them so very much that they will be ever so happy and do the things that they enjoy whatever that may be.

My dear son I hope that this answers your simple question. The answer however is complex yet simple at the same time. I hope I gave you an understanable context in which all of this occurs. I love you.

Yes! You certainly answered my question and gave us children much more beautiful information about the context in which all of this occurs. We all benefit from knowing so much more about our existence and how God's creations work together.

13

The Magnificence of God's Interlocking Creations

As the sacred children of God, our starting point is when our Almighty Father created each of us individually and uniquely from every other child. We were born as spirit beings inside the Heavenly Kingdom. No two children are the same. Our Father created all of us within a blink of an eye as measured by time in the Heavenly Kingdom, which is part of the Spiritual realm.

To many people, this sounds ridiculous. But it is not. Remember, the Holy Trinity exists outside of the timeline we live in on earth. As the Bible says, a day may seem like a thousand years, and a thousand years may seem like a day. Multiple timelines exist, and our Heavenly Father lives in all of them simultaneously at his will.

We were all created as spiritual beings who were living within the Heavenly Kingdom with our Almighty Father. Our Father loves us so much that He spent eons of time with us in the Heavenly Kingdom. We played with our Father during this magnificent era and asked Him many questions. We experienced many magnificent things with Him in the Kingdom, and our Father taught us many wonderful items of truthful knowledge regarding our existence and all other appropriate creations our Father created.

Because our Father exists across all time simultaneously, He knew beforehand that one of his closest angels would rebel against Him. This introduced ugly sin within his creations. Lucifer, the angel, rebelled and was cast out of the Heavenly Kingdom along with one-third of the angelic host that followed Him in the rebellion. Because all the angels and all his sacred children made in his image have the gift of free will, our Father created three additional creations that are listed below.

These are specifically designed to provide a pathway back to our Heavenly Father if we choose to love Him and not succumb to the temptations of Satan, the evil one, while we live on earth. Our Father has given us every chance to return to Him in the Heavenly Kingdom. The physical realm was formed to specifically address, prove, and display to all creation and to ourselves which decision we make. Do we choose God, or do we choose Satan?

GOD PROVIDES HIS SACRED CHILDREN THE OPPORTUNITY TO RETURN TO HIM IN HEAVEN

This next section describes God's magnificent, interlocking, and perfect creations for his sacred children. These will allow those of his children that love Him to be redeemed from sin and live in the Heavenly Kingdom with God Almighty for all eternity. These three separate creations are designed to work closely in concert with each other. Each one is built with the other two in mind. Each one works flawlessly with the other two. If they do not work perfectly together, then God's plan for the salvation of his sacred children will not work.

These three creations are an example of irreducible complexity on a very large scale. They all must work together as a threesome, or nothing will work because one depends on the other for everything to function properly.

Later, I will discuss the scientific concept of "irreducible complexity" and use an example of a Swiss watch to illustrate that point. This is where each separate part of a watch must interact with all the other pieces. Otherwise, the watch will not work. These three perfect creations work together flawlessly for the benefit of God's sacred spiritual children. These three connected creations are:

The physical realm is where one-half of our existence resides. Most people think this is the only existence we have, the physical. But they are completely wrong. Our physical bodies and brain are the home on earth for our real identity, our spirit body.

The spiritual realm is where the other half of our existence resides. Remember, each of us is a spiritual being having a physical experience.

It is never that we are a physical creature, sometimes having a spiritual experience. No, that is not the case at any time.

Our physical bodies are designed to function within the physical realm. The universe and our earth were created specifically to support human life. We must have physical bodies so that we can propagate God's children through the ages. And to live out our spiritual mission on earth.

The interlocking nature of the physical and spiritual realms manifests within our physical bodies. I will discuss in detail how and why our spirit being is so tightly connected to our physical being. Then, I will thoroughly explore how the above three creations interact with each other with magnificent precision. Looking at all three of these creations and how they work together is an astounding plan of God. They provide a wonderful pathway back to our Almighty Father in Heaven if we choose by our free will. It allows us to return to the Heavenly Kingdom where each of us lived for eons.

NOTHING BY CHANCE

There are no coincidences, no accidents of providence regarding all that is seen and unseen in God's creation. Everything you and I come into contact with and think about is a gift from God for our redemption. This is truly the greatest story ever told. All three of the creations discussed above did not just appear magically and started to work together in such a loving and precise manner by pure chance and probability. They were planned and designed to perfection. Remember, in this section about randomness and creation, it would be one chance in 1 to the power of 143rd. There are not that many atoms in the entire cosmos.

Our Trinity designed every aspect of our human body. All the contributing pieces of our bodies link together in uncountable ways to function properly. I will discuss this in detail in a following chapter.

EVOLUTIONISTS & ATHEISTS

What I have just discussed is the truth of what God has revealed. However, within the free will of human minds, things like this will always be resisted and lied about if they do not fit a person's uninformed personal view of life or ambitions. The progressive socialist evolutionists sow cancerous mental seeds about God's creations, saying that everything is a big accident by "random selection." Their attempt is to cancel out the truth of the existence of our Heavenly Trinity. Everything they say regarding things coming into existence by random chance is based on pure atheism and outright denial of Almighty God. There is no better way to condemn yourself to hell.

Has anyone examined the previous phrase, "random selection?" To begin with, it is an oxymoron. The phrase random selection is contradictory to itself. How can something be random yet at the same time perform a process of selection? Think deeply about this. The word selection means that an overarching power must choose one item over another. It also says that some manner of intelligent criteria must guide the selection process to determine what is acceptable and what is not. It also means that some form of intelligence must be present to determine the selection criteria and then have the power to execute the resulting selection process.

Evolutionists work hard to avoid these obvious holes in their beloved Darwinian promotions. Always look under the surface of evolutionist thought, and all you will find is a patchwork of contradicting assertions that are oxymoronic. The propagation of natural selection relies on never really thinking about what it says and its implications. In other words, evolutionists don't want people to question or analyze. They simply believe because they said so. This makes evolutionists a religion. What do you do?

Make an idol of randomness? Don't fall for this twisted evolutionary theory. You will end up looking stupid. Many biology professors certainly do because they are married to a Marxist socialist political philosophy that contradicts itself and goes against the truth of God's creation.

The truth be told, the ONLY explanation for these three creations is that an all-powerful, infinitely intelligent force created them with a specific purpose in mind. Beyond this, a plethora of independent evidence demonstrates that this infinite intelligent Godly force exists. This infinite force is who we call Almighty God.

14

The Dimensions and Structure of Creation

Dear Lord: What dimensions do you live in and how many are there?

We have free will to do what pleases us and we want our children to inherit this as well. The space and dimensions that we live or exist in are endless. There are no limitations. Everything is absolute perfection. [9]

TIME

There was NO beginning. There was no time as we know it in our lives today. Normal empirical experiences do not give us an understanding of time. We do know that time can be flexible. There is no scientific theory or hypothesis on what time is other than to say it can order things in sequence, giving us a sense of what we call time. Some people call time the fourth dimension. However, it is a one-way street.

The arrow of time always points forward. It is true that if you get into a spaceship and travel at the speed of light, relative to your twin brother still on earth, upon your return, you will remain the same age as when you left. But your brother will have aged.

Velocity does reduce the forward progress of time but never reverses it. So, it is true when it is said that Almighty God, also known as the Trinity, live from the alpha to the omega. This means there was no beginning, and

---

[9] Our Father in Heaven created us to expand His pleasure and fulfillment by loving His children and they love Him in return through their free will. He wants His children to "inherit" life in paradise with Him

there will be no end. God's children who choose to live a Holy life with their sins forgiven will live for all eternity with the Trinity in a timeless paradise that God has told me cannot even be imagined by us, his children. He loves us so very much.

DIMENSIONS

Most people think there are three dimensions. This is true. However, it is also true that there is a fourth dimension that we do call time. In my meditations with God, He revealed that many more dimensions exist that we cannot perceive or live in. We will probably never be exposed to these other dimensions God referred to. But I speculate that considering Almighty God is infinite, we are not the only game in town, so to speak. On the other hand, our loving Father and the Trinity occupy all of them whenever they wish. And they may live in different time dimensions as well.

Nothing that we human children can conceive of is impossible for God. Everything is possible. At some point in the timeless past, there was only Almighty God. This means there was the Father, the only begotten Son, and the Holy Spirit, which proceeds from them. I do not know if the dimensions we live in already existed in the timeless past. Or did the Trinity create these in anticipation of creating the spiritual and physical realms? These are what Almighty God's children would need to accommodate their future human bodies.

Remember, the Trinity lives in all times, past, present, and future. Therefore, they have exquisitely detailed information regarding what will happen in our future. Remember, it is our future on our timeline but not God's future. Why? Because God already lives in the future. Is this too hard to understand? Yes, it certainly is! There is no way that we mortal children of our Heavenly Father, could understand this. I think the best we can do is to be aware that this information exists and is correct. Godly faith on our part is also mixed in with what I have just said. I do not understand all of what God has revealed. But as his messenger, He expects me to communicate these thoughts to you, his sacred children.
The Trinity created these three realms before they created all of us sacred children. We were created as spiritual beings. We had no physical bodies after our creation, and we lived for eons of our time with the Trinity. As

stated before, this was a magnificently wonderful time of love, joy, excitement, and learning all about existence and our place in it. During this era of being with our Heavenly Father, I am told that this was a magnificently joyful experience for our Father in Heaven as well.

The dimensions of the realms that the Trinity lives in are endless and have no limitations. Everything is absolute perfection. Our spiritual realm is enormous, far bigger than the physical realm we call the universe. The Almighty revealed to me that Heaven is limitless with total freedom for those who love Him.

15

Almighty God Creates The Spiritual Realms

WHEN WAS THE SPIRITUAL REALM CREATED?

The Bible does not identify exactly when the spiritual realm was created. But there are good clues in the Bible. We know that the spiritual realm was created before most of the angels. Before the creation of the spiritual and physical realms, many angels within the Heavenly Kingdom served all the needs of Almighty God and others within the Kingdom. Other and more numerous angels were created on the "First Day" of creation.

It had to be this way because the angels exist within the spiritual realm so that they can serve as messengers between God and his children and, at times, protect his children from Satan and demons. Satan was an angel of high standing in Heaven, and his name was Lucifer. Lucifer and all the other angels had to be created only after Almighty God created the spiritual realm. God knew in advance that one of his highly deemed angels would rebel against Him seeking the honor and glory that Almighty God rightfully is his. God created the spiritual realm, and a section of this realm was later called hell. This also means that Satan's fall from Heaven occurred after the creation of the spiritual realm but before the first day of creation and, of course, Adam and Eve.

CREATING THE SPIRITUAL REALM

Now, since the spiritual realm was created along with the physical realm, we can see that our Heavenly Father was preparing two creations that every one of his sacred children will need due to Satan's treachery and betrayal. It is not a coincidence that you, I, and every human being on this planet are also created with two major characteristics. We are all both 100% human and 100% spiritual. As spiritual beings, we have a physical human experience while on earth.

Don't get this confused with our Lord and Savior, Jesus Christ. He is 100% God and was 100% human at the same time. We are in no way some kind of God but rather a spiritual being created many eons ago while we were within the Heavenly Kingdom with the Trinity. One hypothesis is that there is no timeline in the spiritual realm. There is a timeline within this physical realm. These two timelines are significantly different than the other.

The Bible tells us, "with the Lord, a day is like a thousand years; a thousand years are like a day". Something to ponder, huh? Consider this evidence. Spirits in the spiritual realm do not age. We age here in the physical realm due to the natural law of entropy across the entire physical universe. The scientific definition of entropy is the measure of randomness and chaos within a closed system. Entropy is tightly connected with the dimension of time. Entropy tends things toward more randomness and chaos and degrades things over time. That is the connection.

To me, who worked as a scientist at NASA in the planetary branch, extrapolating this thought means that our Father in Heaven probably suspended the law of entropy for the spiritual realm. This is the physical law that drives order into disorder. Everything on earth decays and disassembles itself. This law of entropy is the fundamental driving principle that makes everyone age as our numerical age advances.

Being a septuagenarian, I hear people my age constantly complaining about aging and saying things like, "I am falling apart. " Yep! Not so in the spiritual realm. I told you the above timeline issue to stimulate your thinking away from the normal physics we encounter every day, assuming that is all there is. Nope! Lots more in God's creation than almost every one of his children think of. So, this small discussion concludes that the properties in the spiritual realm are very different than in our physical realm.

I did ask God how big the spiritual realm was. He responded by saying, ***it is enormous and much bigger than the physical universe.*** *This occurred around June 9, 2022.* Angels are spirit beings with free will created by God. Remembering that the Heavenly realm, the Heavenly Kingdom, has always existed in eternity for endless time. Said differently, the Heavenly Kingdom always had angels to address the needs and wants of the Trinity. Everything was non-physical.

It was spiritual in every way. When God created the spiritual realm so that his sacred children could communicate with Him, He created an abundance of angels to minister to his children, to bring messages to his children, and to assist in a myriad of different ways to help his children understand why they exist in the physical realm.

It was created so the sin-stained children of God could have the opportunity to live with our Heavenly Father in eternal paradise. He is such a loving Father we have that He would go to extreme lengths so we have a chance to live with Him forever in paradise. I suggest you go out at night somewhere there is minimal light pollution from a city and look at all the stars in the sky. What you see is only a tiny fraction of what God created for you to decide through free will to love God or not.

Loving God and living by his rules allow his sacred children to rejoin Him in the Heavenly Kingdom. All his loving children that choose to live a Holy life will live with Him in such a magnificent paradise for all eternity. All you have to do is say YES to Him and NO to Satan. Last note. When we say forever, does that mean God decided to shut off the dimension of time? Something else to ponder.

PERSONAL SPIRITUAL COMMUNICATIONS BETWEEN GOD AND HIS CHILDREN
The divine connection between God and his human children that love Him and the other two members of the Trinity resides in the spiritual realm. Our bodies manifest that perfectly within our brains as they are completely capable of co-residing in both realms at the same time. Thus, we can, as human beings, communicate with our Heavenly Almighty Father while we exist in the physical realm and the spiritual together.
This is an enormous and wonderful capability for every child of Almighty God. It is the special meeting place between God and his sacred children. If a child of God does not love God, it becomes impossible for them to communicate with Him because that child of God cut off communication. These children rule out any loving relationship with Almighty God. They think that all of the above is complete foolishness. But I tell you that I, Richard Ferguson, can converse with my Creator, ask Him questions and

solicit his advice regarding a decision I must make. Our Heavenly Father is listening every instant of our lives.

On this point, for a moment, I form my thoughts within the English language. However, English is not God's native tongue, as you can well imagine. Rather, through many experiences communicating with the Trinity, I discern that God forms a thought in my mind as his response, and it is my mind that translates that instantly into English that I can understand. I do not hear voices, and I do not communicate with God through that mechanism.

Rather through the spiritual part of me, God "talks" a silent language of thought in my brain. Then my brain converts that thought into English. This is the best way I can explain the internal communication between the child of God and God himself. There are many other ways that God can use to speak to his children. It would be a wonderful idea for each of you to get hold of a book with the theme of "Hearing God by Peter Lord" and "The Prophetic Voice of God" by Lana Vawser. My message here is that YES, you can talk to God yourself with no fear but rather joy and happiness.

And when Almighty God wishes to tell me something, He simply breaks into whatever I am doing and tells me what He wants to say. Remember, all things happen according to God's will and his time. This has happened to me on a number of occasions. While writing this book, I hear our Heavenly Father break into my consciousness and tell me something about how He wants this book to be written. All of this communication is spirit to spirit, also called telepathic. How else can it be? It is all based on his love for his children, which He created so long ago.

Mankind has known about the spiritual realm for a long time. It is the realm of spirits that are formed energy. The spiritual realm has been described as "higher" than the physical realm. This is not really true. The spiritual realm overlaps and is intertwined with the physical realm. The evidence of this can be discerned all the time. This is the realm of both God's angels and Lucifer, the fallen angel now known as Satan. Other fallen angels are known now as demons. All exist in this realm. So too, do the Angels that are assigned to protect us from demons and so on. All of us indeed have a guardian angel.

The spiritual realm is also home to the Trinity. However, they live in a very special place called Heaven. The Trinity is all-powerful and can do anything and be anywhere they choose. To be precise, the Trinity is within every particle of existence in all creation. There is nothing that exists outside of the Trinity.

It is this realm that allows our soul's connection with God. I can testify personally that this is ever so true. I wrote a book on this topic that documents my many experiences regarding the spiritual realm. It is titled "The Divine Resting on My Shoulder." I have had hundreds of spiritual experiences in my life, and they continue to this day.

I already described what life was like for God and the Trinity before creation. The Trinity decided to create children in their own image with free will. God knew that there would be trouble in the future because of Lucifer's coming rebellion. They also knew that their sacred children would fall from grace and become sinful. This is because all his children have free will and will succumb to the luring temptations of Satan. This is why almighty God created three separate realms. All this is needed by God's children to provide us with a pathway back to the Heavenly Kingdom from where we came from.

Almighty God created multiple realms, physical and spiritual, so that his children would have a chance to live with Him in paradise for all eternity. Since the existence of God transcends all dimensions, including different dimensions of time, He knew that after He created the angels and his children, a number of things would happen due to Satan and the gift of free will.

THE SPIRITUAL REALM IS WHERE SATAN AFFECTS GOD'S CHILDREN.

There is a real danger for all people where Satan will use the power of spiritual things to deceive us for his evil purposes. Many people succumb to such things as sorcery, crystal balls, witchcraft, astrology, horoscopes, and magic. This usually happens to people with low IQs in backward cultures and societies. All of this is so far away from the truth of loving Christianity. Also, Satan can affect the human mind provided the child of God allow this either consciously or unconsciously. This is pure treachery. <u>Again, this is because our minds are directly connected to the spiritual realm.</u>

Because of my Christian spiritual activities, like writing this book and the six previous spiritual books I have written, I am a big target for Satan and his miserable demons. Satan hates me so very much. In the book I mentioned above, I discuss my encounters with Satan's demons. Truth be told, I have to fight Satan's demons every day of my life. They continually harassed me in the form of distractions and vulgar language hurled at me in their effort to stop me from focusing and writing this book and the others I have written.

The good news is that I do have the spiritual power to get rid of them by commanding them to go back to hell, where they belong, in the name of our Lord and Savior, Jesus Christ. Each and every one of us Christians has the same power I just described. You also can command Satan and his demons to leave you instantly in the name of our Lord and Savior, Jesus Christ. I use the imagery of a huge flame thrower aimed at them, and away they go. But all of this is such a distraction and nuisance that it is really irritating.

On another level, there are far more sophisticated ways that Satan tries to get to people. He can make something that is destructive look very attractive to people according to their personality and desires. Think alcohol and drugs. In this way, He constructs temptations in hopes of luring people to sin. Whole books can be written on this topic, but I think you have the idea for now.

But do not fear Satan and his demons. He cannot force you to do something you do not want to do. He works by enticement and pleasure with sinful hidden hooks attached to whatever he offers. Always pray for God's protection and guidance in all things, and you will be just fine.

A SHORT HISTORY

Next is a short history of key events. Not everything is included, though. I will describe all the details later. God created these multiple realms before Satan's rebellion. Why? Remember that God exists outside of time, and He knows everything that will happen in the future. God was planning ahead because He knew his children would need these realms for their salvation so as to return to Him in the Heavenly Kingdom. Were it not for Satan's rebellion, these realms would be unnecessary. Hell was also created as a part of the spiritual realm that has no escape. However, Satan being an angel, can come and go as He pleases. So too, can his demons.

Lucifer, one of the highest and most powerful angels, rebelled against God by trying to overthrow Him from his rightful throne. Pride was found within Lucifer. This was his fateful downfall. Lucifer would take one-third of the angels with Him during the rebellion. There would be a battle and conflict in the Heavenly realm. All of this happened in a blink of an eye.

Lucifer instantly lost this war, was cast down from the Heavenly realm forever, and became the prince of this earth. Lucifer, now Satan, however, would still have access to Heaven. He and his demons would then dwell in a place called many names like Hades, Sheol, Gehenna, Hell, and finally, Tophet. Yet He also has access to the spiritual realm, which God's children also have access to. Ultimately, because of a physical force known as entropy, Satan and everything aligned with Him will slowly come apart and evaporate back into the nothingness from which they were created by Almighty God.

Speaking of hell, if a child of God is sent to that place, there is no escape for them. They made their choice. There is no such thing as parole. After God created his children, we spent many eons of time with our Father in the Heavenly Kingdom. There we would have glorious times of joy, love, and fulfillment, along with great learnings about our Father and all of his creations. Only much later, after our creation, would we begin to be born into the physical realm on earth.

Earth is a very special place created within a special physical universe, so his children could decide if they wanted to join God in eternal paradise or live in hell with Satan. Before we were born here on earth, we knew that choosing Satan would mean our ultimate extinction and dissolution into nothingness. However, before we were born on earth, we were made to forget all our Heavenly experiences and knowledge. This is because God wanted only his children, that chose Him with their free will to love Him and reject Satan. Not knowing what it was like for us while we lived in the Kingdom would allow us to reveal our true selves and not be biased by our knowledge of Heaven.

Now Satan and his demons spend all their time plotting many different ways to trick, encourage and deceive as many of God's children as they can on earth, so they commit acts of sin. This is because they reject God and his Holy, loving ways. Rejecting God results in these children going to hell. They think that causing suffering and pain to God's children will somehow make their existence more pleasant. This is not mythology. It is bone-breaking real in every sense. Satan conducts his rebellion and attacks against God's sacred children in the spiritual realm. And the spiritual realm exists within our spiritual selves hosted within our brains.

This brings us up to the present time, where all of us are engaged in a cosmic spiritual war with Satan and his demons. Later in a subsequent section, I will discuss in detail the nature of spiritual warfare and how all Christians can succeed in winning.

WHY A CREATION OF THE SPIRITUAL AND PHYSICAL REALM TOGETHER?

For his children to work out their redemption in the physical world, we need God's active guidance and support; as said before, this is through the spiritual realm. The physical realm gives God's children instant feedback on the goodness or badness of their actions in this physical realm. This is how we learn our faults and strengths to adjust them to improve ourselves according to the will of our Father. Then we can someday enter the Heavenly Kingdom.

Our spirits within our physical bodies are connected within each of us. This is where the spiritual realm is tightly connected with the physical realm. They interact with each other inside our heads. This most important connection occurs within our minds and is projected outward into the physical and spiritual realms. It is this sacred connection that allows physical events and the choices we make to affect our spiritual makeup. This is ever so much an extremely important fact to remember. Our bodies contain the holy connection between the spiritual and physical realms inside our minds.

OUR HEAVENLY FATHER EXISTS WITHIN AND THROUGHOUT ALL CREATION

Most people, including Christians, think, "I am here, and God is out there somewhere." Well, this is completely wrong. Almighty God is everywhere. He resides in every aspect of his creations. This includes us, his sacred children. We were created by our Father. Therefore, God resides within each and every one of us. He is within us. Some people call that our conscience. Since God is completely spirit, He resides within our minds. That is where we have our connection with the spiritual realm and God. It is impossible for us to ever hide from God or keep secrets from our Heavenly Father or the other two members of the Trinity.

Almost all people, including Christians, do not realize the fact that Almighty God resides throughout his creations. St. Paul realized this when no matter where he went in his travels, God was there. He wrote about this in one of his letters to an early church. Our Heavenly Father can be found in every part of his creations. Therefore, it is consistent that God can even be found within our minds, the spiritual part of ourselves. This means that the Trinity knows each one of us in magnificent detail. God knows every thought we have, every intention and emotion, etc. There are no secrets within the spiritual realm, NONE!

Pity the crooks and politicians. They think they can hide their nefarious deeds from everyone. Nope! They cannot hide anything from our Father and the Trinity. Every minute detail is plain to see for them. When their time comes, imagine what a shock this will be to these dishonest Satanic beings.

With Almighty God within each of us, we can forget what we Catholic School refugees were taught. That when we pray, those prayers need to ascend up into Heaven. We must be good little boys and girls if we want God to hear our prayers. Nope! That is pure BS. God is already aware of what it is that we will pray about. All of us are number one in God's priority list.

THE SPIRITUAL AND PHYSICAL REALMS WORK TOGETHER

The combination of the spiritual realm and earth is the special meeting place between God and His sacred children. The divine connection between God and his human children that love Him and the other two members of the Trinity resides within the spiritual realm and the spiritual part of us. We manifest that perfectly within our physical bodies and our minds, as they are completely capable of co-residing in both realms at the same time.

Thus, as humans, we can communicate with our Heavenly Almighty Father while we exist in the physical and spiritual realms. This is an enormous and wonderful sacred gift and capability for every child of Almighty God. All too often, these sacred gifts are ignored and taken for granted. For those children that have fallen into Satan's influence, the thought that we are naturally connected to God is completely avoided and rejected. Progressives call this a "vast right-wing conspiracy."

The spiritual realm is also home to the Trinity, more precisely, the Heavenly Kingdom, a very special place within the spiritual realm, a very special place called Heaven. I should point out that the Heavenly realm exists within the enormous spiritual realm. However, it is a place that is heavily guarded and has different characteristics from the general spiritual realm. One can go there <u>only with specific permission</u> from Almighty God. It is this realm that allows our spirit's connection with God. I can testify personally that this is ever so true. I wrote a book on this topic that documents many experiences I have had in my life regarding the spiritual realm. One time I was taken to Heaven and given a detailed tour of my future house by my late wife, Marilyn. It is documented in one of my previous spiritual books. It is titled "The Divine Resting on My Shoulder."

You can consider that each of our spirits, yours and mine, have a direct connection to God through the spiritual realm. This is Biblical.

Now may the God of peace Himself sanctify you completely; and may your whole spirit, soul, and body be preserved blameless at the coming of our Lord Jesus Christ. [10]

---

[10] 1Thess. 5:23

THE PARALLEL CHARACTER WE HAVE WITH JESUS

Jesus was 100% human and, at the same time, 100% God. God is 100% spiritual. You will never see our Heavenly Father walking down the street. From this, we can see that our nature and design by our Father in Heaven is 100% human, with our 100% internal spirit having direct connections with the spiritual realm meaning the Holy Trinity. Remember also that the Trinity is spiritual and operates within the spiritual realm we are connected to.

The beauty of this is that within our minds resides our spiritual connection, and therefore the Heavenly Trinity is here with us 100% of the time. This is even when we do not even notice it. But our Father, our Lord and Savior, and the Holy Spirit which proceeds from them are with us all the time. Just how wonderful is that?

This is one way that it works. If you decide to act out in the physical a deed that results in pain for another person, your spiritual health is negatively affected, and that deed is recorded within the spiritual realm forever. This is also true for everything good and loving that you do on earth as well. Most people never know that everything you say and do, everything you think, your attitudes, your intentions, and your emotions are all recorded to the last detail in the spiritual realm via its connection to you in the physical realm or universe.

Doing something negative adds to any separation that you may have with our Lord Jesus Christ, along with Almighty God and the Holy Spirit. Additionally, within the spiritual realm, there exists records of every deed that has ever been done or spoken for every person that ever existed. Some people call them Akashic records.

The Akashic records are a compendium of all universal events, thoughts, words, emotions, and intent ever to have occurred across all of God's creation. In my prayers I have asked our Heavenly Father if these records actually exist. Our Father's response was very clear and to the point. God said, "YES". This is what He said directly to me.

Oh my, this is ever so important because absolutely everything you have thought, intended, said, and done is recorded in detail forever. To those who think they can hide something, they are completely wrong and in for a monumental shock when they are confronted after their death with everything they have ever done in their life. Conversely, whenever a person does something good, the thoughts and motivations that precede the physical action in this world are also recorded forever.

A REAL STORY WITH ME USING THE AKASHIC RECORDS

You may wonder how this is manifested in God's Heavenly Kingdom. I will tell you a story about the time I was taken out of my body, and my late wife Marilyn asked me if I wanted to see my future house in Heaven. Well, that certainly got my attention. I said yes. In another book that I wrote titled, "The Divine Resting On My Shoulder," I tell the story of my late wife giving me a tour of my Heavenly home. I will not get into the details here.

Instead, I want to focus on a history book that was in my house. This book was very large and in the library. There were many books in my library, and I can only imagine that other books like this contained pictures that I could also dive into and experience. This particular book contained both text and very large pictures of events in human history. As I paged through it, looking at the different pictures, I came to understand that I could take myself into a historical picture and become part of the action shown in that picture and experience exactly what was going on firsthand.

It was as if I was indeed living in the action and event depicted by that picture. Somehow, every little detail of what was occurring at the time of this picture was recorded and stored forever so that people in Heaven like me could explore in the greatest detail what historical events had occurred in their life or any other time and place.

This can only be done by some mechanism I do not understand, recording and storing into a huge archive. And then give people the opportunity to re-experience any event that they choose. Or they can experience any event and place they would like to experience in the past. Think about this, my dear child of God, and consider the implications of what I have just said. If you want, you can relive your entire life that you are living right now.

The list of things you can do is absolutely amazing and endless. I explain this in more detail in other places in this book, but to summarize, the spiritual realm that surrounds us and the physical realm is a duality that we live in. Our bodies similarly are both physical and spiritual. This is wonderful because God's children can use the physical part of our bodies to reproduce over a very long time, and we can use our spiritual part to stay in constant communication with our loving Almighty Father in Heaven. More on this in another section of this book.

16

Almighty God Creates The Physical Realm

WHY GOD CREATED THIS PHYSICAL UNIVERSE

What a magnificent story of God's love for his future creations (yes, more than we know about) and how He thoughtfully prepared everything to such fantastic precision for the benefit of his children. This is the magnificent and great love story of a Father to his children. It is indeed a love story of our almighty and loving Father. He wished, with the other two members of the Trinity, to expand their personal enjoyment and fulfillment by having sacred children that would love them through their own free will.

Their choice to love our Heavenly Father must be through his children's free will. For Almighty God will not force anyone into something they do not choose. If anything, if it is forced, it cannot be love. God is the essence of love. To love our Heavenly Father must be through free will. It can never be forced on any of his sacred children.

As said earlier, God lived in perfect community, love, and companionship with his Holy Spirit and His only begotten son for timeless eons. Remember that there are three distinct aspects of Almighty God, all one in being. God our Father, the Holy Spirit, and his only begotten son decided to expand their existence by creating sacred children that were made in their Holy image. Love drove the expansion of God's being into creating his children with the wonderful gift of free will. This is so God can love them and be loved in return by his children, who choose through their free will to love Him in return. This can only increase his great contentment and fulfillment within his boundless, eternal existence.

It is extremely important that every child of God know and understand that you and I are the focus of all creation. Every bit of every creation

God has brought into existence was and is for the benefit of his sacred human children. Do not ever forget this.

Our Heavenly Father loves us, his sacred children, so much that He created two major realms of existence that have only one purpose. To give all his children with their bi-dimensional bodies a chance to return to Him in Heavenly paradise and live together for all eternity.

God did create all that you are going to read about for the express benefit of you and me so that we can spend eternity with our loving Father in Heaven if we so choose. It is a terrible shame that so many people today do not understand this and continue to reject our Almighty Father in Heaven. Also, remember that the road to the Heavenly Kingdom is narrow, and the road to Satan's place is wide.

MANY DIFFERENT TYPES OF GOD'S CHILDREN

In my encounters with people, I have found that many do believe in our Heavenly Father and the teachings of our Lord Jesus Christ, acting in a loving manner. There are others that follow their conscience, which was given to them by our Heavenly Father as a moral guide for our life. This is one way of expressing love for our Father in Heaven. But then also, I have encountered people that don't care one way or the other about the existence of God.

They bumble along through life, never making the connection between Godly teachings of life and their lives themselves. Others do not believe God exists; they are the atheists among us. They tend to be very defensive in the presence of believers. Lastly, there is a belligerent bunch of people that consciously, actively, knowingly, willfully, and completely reject Almighty God and his love for them. These people will attack Christians or other believers in many different ways.

One very telling signpost of this active rejection of God are spoken phrases they may say, like, "I will do things my way." I have experienced this kind of antagonistic behavior more than once. I pity those people. Because when their day comes, every inkling of their thoughts, attitudes, and emotions against God and Christians alike will be shown to them by Heavenly-loving angels after they pass away. They will be held accountable for all of it, all their attitudes and behaviors, whether they be good or bad. Also, everything good and loving that a child of God does and says is also revealed. And it will go very well for their entry back into the Heavenly Kingdom.

All of God's children, you and me, are made in his image within the spiritual and physical realms. But, before God thought our physical universe into existence, He had to prepare many things for us. He brought into existence the physical universe we know and live in today. Remember, Almighty God exists across the entire timeline on which our universe has been created. So, He knows what will happen before it does.

He knew of the coming rebellion of Lucifer, knew his children would fall into sin, and He decided to save them from sin and redeem them so they could live with Him in paradise for all eternity. But it is up to God's sacred children's free will whether to accept God's offer or not. Remember that our Heavenly Father created us within a blink of an eye. He made each one of us completely unique and different from every other sacred child of his.

All his children stayed within the Heavenly Kingdom for uncountable eons of time. We played with our loving Father and each other, which held such delicious, fulfilling, and joyful experiences for us. During that time with our Father, He educated us on many aspects of the Trinity's existence and how we fit into all of that. We all knew we would have a decision to make. To love God and, through our free will, choose our Heavenly Father so we may spend all eternity with Him in the Heavenly Kingdom or choose Satan, succumb to his temptations, and live a life of evil.

Doing that would result in hell for us and ultimately complete dissolution back into the nothingness from which we came. The above different types of people and their variations are brought on by many different factors in people's lives. But the common denominator is their free will choices.

A WONDROUS MEETING PLACE FOR THE CHILDREN OF GOD

When you look up at the sky and see billions of stars, you only see a tiny fraction of what God has created for all of us, children of his. For it takes not only the stars that you can see, but astrophysics, astronomy, and other sciences tell us that the interaction of billions of galaxies that you cannot see are responsible for creating the conditions that allow our earth to remain stable enough for a long enough period of time to support human life.

We also know that this period of time is soon coming to an end because of the galactic cycles that prevail. All of this is in the plans of Almighty God. We have great astronomers like Dr. Hugh Ross and many others that think about this for their marvelous work that informs us as to the timing of the cycles of life. I suggest you read some of his books at books@reason.org. One book, in particular, is titled "The Improbable Planet." It describes our beloved earth and all the Galactic requirements for the earth to exist and support human life. I will give just a few details in the next section.

Our physical universe is a shining example of an extremely complex system of interlocking influences, connections, and other codependent processes that provide the necessary conditions for a planet like earth to exist. Not only to exist but to exist for a long enough time from a biological and physical perspective that supports human life and accomplishes what God wants for his children while they're on earth. These interlocking processes and dependencies across the universe provide a huge framework that holds the earth in the proper position so that when God created humans, they could propagate and pass along their heritage to subsequent generations.

This is so that all of God's children can come to earth, discover themselves and decide through attitudes, emotions, and actions that will determine whether they will spend eternity in the Heavenly Kingdom with their Father or go to hell and spend time with Satan and his demons. This will be before they are dissolved into nothingness by means of entropy from which they came. All these physical processes and codependency's can be described in a scientific term known as irreducible complexity.

IRREDUCIBLE COMPLEXITY:

The creation of the physical realm is an absolutely magnificent piece of design and interlocking irreducible complexity that the human mind cannot completely understand. Before we go any further, I need to define the meaning of the phrase "irreducible complexity." It simply means a term used to describe a characteristic of certain complex systems whereby they need all of their individual component parts in place to function properly.

Remove one part of an irreducibly complex system, and the whole thing ceases to function. Our physical universe is one gigantic set of interlocking relationships, each of which are in and of themselves extraordinarily large irreducible complex systems.

It is impossible to reduce the complexity of, simplify an irreducibly complex system by removing any of its component parts and still maintain its functionality. Perhaps a Swiss watch is a good example. Just take out one spring or gear, and it does not work anymore. This scientific observation applies to many thousands of Galactic interactions necessary to be implemented with unbelievable accuracy and precision that it's hard to imagine. But it is all true. Mess with the universe and the interlocking relationships will fall apart, causing the earth to not support human life as God requires.

Now, in the physical universe, you can remove a few solar systems here and there or a galaxy, and not much would happen. But if you tinker a little too much, you will throw off the finely tuned balance of the entire cosmos to the point where the earth would not be stable enough to sustain human life long enough for God's sacred children to make the simple choice of God or Satan.

There must be sufficient cosmic stability for God's children. The human race will not be able to develop and have enough time to realize who we are and make our grand choice that God intends for us to make. This grand choice is simple, do we choose eternal life with our Heavenly Father, or do we choose to go and do things our own way? The latter choice means that as we were created out of nothing, those who reject the love of Almighty God will return to nothingness.

It is with the same irreducible complexity and mind-boggling precision that is also necessary for our created human bodies to function and support our physical existence and spiritual connections. The amount of irreducible complex relationships within our bodies is many multiples of thousands upon thousands.

There is not one part of our physical bodies that is not deeply involved in irreducibly complex relationships with other parts of our bodies. There is absolutely zero chance that our bodies happened through random chance development due to the vast array of complex systems in our bodies. People who believe in evolution have not thought about it in the slightest. If so, the depth of their analysis is no deeper than a cheap paint job on a rusted-out 1957 Chevy stored in a junkyard somewhere.

Sorry, Darwin, you did very good botany on your ship, the HMS Beagle. You produced a very nice theory, but as you said in your book *The Origin Of Species*, if it can be shown that life did not progress in tiny increments over a very long length of time, then my theory is wrong. I salute you, Prof. Darwin, for being so very objective and honest in the science you conducted. Little did you know that much later, wacko liberal Democrats have co-opted your remarkable work into a political action committee that distorts everything in sight. This is so they will hopefully fool enough of the people to retain political power over everybody else's lives.

The good news, however, is that our scientists in astronomy, astrophysics, chemistry, and other deep scientific disciplines have been studying our universe for hundreds of years. It is a magnificent achievement for us to have accomplished sufficient scientific knowledge that we may now be able to examine the cosmos to confirm that it is impossible for the cosmos to form itself out of nothingness. This is so even if some prominent scientists think our universe created itself.

Sorry Prof. Hawking, the universe never was and never will be able to explode itself out of nothingness due to a big random quantum fluctuation. Good grief Prof. Hawking, we both know that natural quantum fluctuations cannot have the necessary energy to explode into the whole cosmos. ONLY something outside our purview where God exists can do that. This is what one of your last papers promoted. Interviewed by the Guardian, he said, "I regard the brain as a computer which will stop working when its components fail" also he said, he told the *Guardian.* "There is no Heaven or afterlife for broken down computers; that is a fairy story for people afraid of the dark."..., we would know everything that God would know if there were a God, which there isn't. I'm an atheist." It is also too bad that you are an atheist, Dr. Hawking. It biased your magnificent scientific career. Besides, your argument falls apart completely if you shine light on it.

The Creation of the Physical Universe

As hard as it may seem for us, God's sacred children were thought into existence in the blink of an eye. Remember that Almighty God lives in many different time dimensions simultaneously. The Bible describes one day in Heaven as a thousand years on earth. We can only imagine what time must translate like in the other dimensions that Almighty God occupies. But from our perspective in our universe, our physical universe began approximately 13.8 billion years ago from a very hot point of something beyond plasma. It began expanding faster than what we call the speed of light. Astrophysicists call this the period of inflation.

Scientists today have an enormously complete understanding of our universe all the way back until the universe was only 10 X-43rd seconds old. To put this into perspective, this number looks like this:

.0000000000000000000000000000000000000000001 seconds

This is completely amazing to think that we have scientists today that have a wonderful grasp of what God did in the creation of the physical universe. We know what the universe was like so ever close to the instant the universe began to be born. Any closer than this 10 X 43rd second before, the math breaks down and becomes determinative.

There is an exciting statistic about the first moment of physical creation. Max Plank, the renowned physicist, calculated that the temperature of the tiny sphere from which everything physical came from was 1.416×10 to the 32nd power. According to science, that is the maximum temperature possible in any physical structure. You should remember this number because <u>it also means that time began when the universe began.</u>

In the book "*The Creator and The Cosmos*" by Dr. Hugh Ross Ph. D., He wrote, "of all the Holy books of the religions of the world, <u>only the Bible unambiguously states that time is finite</u>, that time has a beginning, that God created time, that God is capable of cause and effect operations before the time dimension of the universe existed, and that God did cause many effects before the time component of our universe existed.

After a time, our physical universe continued to increase in size and cool down from enormous temperatures. Then atoms and then molecules started to form. Then according to the laws of chemistry, molecules and then more complex molecules started to form. Then far more complex minerals started to form. And then, because of the laws of gravity, very large bodies of matter began to form, and because these large bodies of matter and velocity to them they started to spin around each other some of these large bodies of matter became so large that they compressed. Their insides got so hot that they triggered nuclear fusion reactions and started to give off enormous amounts of heat, and today we call those globs of extremely hot spinning matter which are stars.

Huge areas of the cosmos became homes of billions and billions of stars which we now call galaxies. The star's lifetimes stretch into billions of years. Then after a time, more globs of stars, through gravity, started spinning around themselves, informed spiral galaxies. We call the galaxy we live in the Milky Way. There are billions more galaxies in the visible universe.

You would think this process of forming stars and then forming galaxies would be quite random, but you would be wrong. Early in this process, because of quantum fluctuations, you would find that it was far more a clumpy sort of arrangement where globs of stars would attract each other and leave large holes here and there, or there would hardly be any stars and subsequent galaxies. Over more periods of time, something very

115

strange occurred that our scientists are puzzled about today, which is the appearance of what is called dark energy and dark matter. Scientists do not understand what it is.

We know it is there, but we cannot measure it directly. Only by the effect it has on the matter that we can see. I talked about entropy, and that hell is entropy running wild which is actually what we are seeing at the outskirts of our physical universe. As we speak, we see fewer and fewer stars as they disappear into the distance. If this continues, the visible universe that we see will become smaller and smaller and smaller to the point where it will be only the earth that we see, and then finally our earth will dissolve as well into nothingness. But for those who believe in our Almighty Father, we will be in timeless eternity with infinite fulfillment with our Father in Heaven, and the physicality of the universe will in no way affect us at all.

Everything I talked about led to our night sky blessed with ever so many beautiful star formations and the Milky Way. Away from light pollution and smog out in the open in very dark areas, you can see the Milky Way as a band of dense stars that run across the sky from one into the other. I saw this when I was on a cruise ship in the middle of the Atlantic Ocean. The captain was kind enough to shut off the upper deck lights, so it was perfect conditions to see God's magnificent creation right in front of my eyes and the group of people I was with. And to think some people in science believe all of it was a random event of a quantum fluctuation.

That is just plain BS. Being a scientist does not prove you are correct. The truth of everything is available to the children of God that believe in the Lord Jesus Christ and our Almighty Father in Heaven along with their Holy Spirit, which proceeds from them.

Remember these key points:

- I have discussed the creation of the physical realm that we refer to as the universe. It did have a finite starting point along with the dimension of time. The common understanding is that the universe began 13.7 billion years ago based on our timeline.

- This physical realm allows our bodies to host our Heavenly spirits within them, allowing God's children to interact directly with the spiritual realm.

- This interaction occurs within our minds/spiritual bodies. It is our minds that determine the actions we take in the physical realm. That is acted out with our physical bodies. Our physical actions in the physical realm broadcasts to the world and the spiritual realm what is inside our minds and spirit.

- What we do within the physical directly affects our minds, spirit, and others of God's children around us.

- The results of our actions give us feedback on the value system and other characteristics in our minds and, most importantly, within our spirits.

- The smart person will use this physical realm feedback to change what is contained within their minds and spiritual being. In this way, we can consciously move closer and closer to Almighty God and his divine will for us.

- Without the physical realm, we would not be able to change and would not be able to overcome our sinful nature.

- Only within the physical realm allows us to change ourselves and our spiritual beings. God can meet us one-on-one within our spiritual minds while we remain in the physical realm for a time. Here, we can confess our sins to our Almighty Father and ask for his forgiveness and guidance in what we say and do for the rest of our lives. If we are sincere in our spiritual hearts in asking for forgiveness and his guidance, then I believe our Father will certainly forgive you of your sins. In doing so, you have become a new creation.

- The spiritual and physical realms have been carefully crafted by our Almighty Father to connect with our physical bodies and our spiritual minds. Without this creation, we would have no opportunity to choose our Father and spend all eternity with Him in a paradise that is beyond our imagination while on earth.

- The physical part of our existence and our physical bodies are designed to propagate God's children throughout many generations. This is necessary because there are far more of God's spiritual children waiting in the Heavenly realm than would fit on this planet all at once. They wait for their opportunity to come to earth and live their life to choose (with our free will) our Almighty Father over Satan and live in paradise with Him.

- Before God's only begotten son, our Lord and Savior Jesus Christ, came to earth, there was no connection between God's children on earth and our Heavenly Father. Jesus Christ restored this Holy connection so that once we chose our Heavenly Father, we would ascend back from where we came, which is from the Heavenly Kingdom. Rejecting our Lord Jesus Christ dooms that person to a very shortened existence as entropy ultimately dissolves them back into the nothingness from where they came. It must be this way, for the alternative is to allow sin back into the Holy Kingdom. That cannot and will not ever happen.

Now let us proceed to a detailed examination of what it took for God to create the physical realm we call the universe. It is far more complex than we can imagine because of all the intricate systems within the universe of irreducible complexity. The mechanisms within our universe have many tightly bound parameters that, if not there, the universe would not be able to support a singular planet called Earth and support human life, which is the will of God.

17

The Holy Spirit And Creation

Within the Bible and other Biblical literature, when it comes to the topic of creation, all of us attribute creation to Almighty God. This is completely correct. For Almighty God has created everything seen and unseen. But we as Christians must continue to remember that our Father in Heaven is also described as a Trinity of three members, each of which is infinite and all-powerful in their own right.

Remember earlier in this book when I described in more detail the attributes of the members within the Trinity and how they explored and created different things together and explored each other's infinite character to their magnificent joy and fulfillment?

But the Holy Spirit, which proceeds from Almighty God, also had a direct role in creating all the realms of existence that we, God's children, are aware of. This is something that we need to not forget.

Regarding our Holy Spirit, He played a vital role in creating the spiritual realm, the physical realm, and us, God's children.

August 9, 2022, 7:55 AM
Our Loving Almighty Father

Our Holy Spirit was indeed intimately involved with the creation of what is said above. He brought to our creation, a sense of equity and fairness that our children will learn from within their experience in the physical realm. Everything in creation is in perfect balance and harmony. Remember all of creation, every particle of it, was created out of complete nothingness.

It is your Holy Spirit, our Holy Spirit that proceeded from the true entity to ensure that all creation was in equilibrium. This is a form of fairness and it also brings forth that when something occurs either naturally or man-made, feedback from a violation of equality, immediately presents itself and forces of the universe act upon it to bring it back into the balance and equity that your Father in Heaven has commanded.

It is the Holy Spirit that has created the organizing forces and structures that hold all things together that have been created by our Father in Heaven. It is these forces that again have created balance and equilibrium that you as our children never once even think about. And that is okay because your Father in Heaven has provided this for you through the Holy Spirit so that you may participate in walking up the pathway toward the Heavenly realm and live forever, eternally, with us in the Trinity and most notably your Father, your Almighty Father, in Heaven and in a paradise that exceeds by far anything your minds can imagine.

Out of nothingness my dear son, the forces of balance, equity, fairness, and equilibrium has been created by your Father in Heaven within the auspices of our Holy Spirit.

It is also true that when each of our children are born into the physical realm on earth, you are born with a sense of fairness and equality. When a very small child interacts with another, if the other violates this fairness by taking away a toy, there is instant reaction to this incident disequilibrium and concept of ownership that is inborn within our children comes into play. When the child lost its toy immediately takes action to retrieve that to restore the previous balance. It is this kind of thing that is a magnificent force that applies to all creation, seen and unseen.

When the planets revolve around each other and equilibrium this did not happen by chance, rather it happened by design. Some people call this Mother nature working. This is a primitive way of saying and recognizing the balancing of all things seen and unseen within all creation. Every phenomenon always seeks balance in one way or another. It is what mankind's laws are all about at its root. My dear son I hope this answers your question about our Holy Spirit and its overarching role in the creation of all that is seen and unseen. Lastly there is more that the Holy Spirit has done that you will not understand. I love you.

I hope, dear reader, that the above will show some of the details and Almighty power that the Holy Spirit holds within the Trinity to benefit all of us who are God's children. Remember that everything within existence, with all the laws, with all the forces and attractions in creation, have come from nothingness. Nothingness means that even the slightest shred of balance and equilibrium does not exist.

Regarding nothingness, this is something that our human minds cannot fully grasp. Nothingness means the absence of anything at all. Most people think of nothingness as blackness. It is not, for blackness in and of itself is something. Therefore, it cannot be nothingness. There is no dimensionality about nothingness. There is not the slightest particle of existence within nothingness, for that would be something. Our sciences have produced the wonderment of information and better lives for God's children. But science can never approach what nothingness is.

I hope this gives you a flavor and some insight that in some way approaches the idea of nothingness, for nothingness is what all existence came from due to the love and action of our Holy Father in Heaven. All existence that surrounds us in any way has been created by our Almighty Father in Heaven with the other members of the Trinity. If not, there would be nothingness.

18

Advanced Science Proves God is the Creator

THESE SCIENTIFIC DISCOVERIES PROVE GOD IS THE CREATOR

This title says it all. If Almighty God did create all that is seen and unseen, as the New Testament says, it is unavoidable that his creation will have his fingerprints all over it. And science today is now actively discovering just how deep our Heavenly Father's fingerprints are in this physical creation we call the universe. There is a huge pot full of cosmic parameters that must be exactly right, a tiny bit too big, no good, a tiny bit too small, no good. Everything must be fine-tuned way beyond the accuracy of the finest Swiss watch, even though we are talking about something huge like the universe. And our Heavenly Father designed things and crafted them to these kinds of accuracies.

That's what this section is all about. It is showing you a glimpse, not a complete dissertation, but a glimpse of the significant number of parameters that must be specific values for our universe to support us, God's children on planet earth. And those specific scientific values are exactly where they should be for humans to be here on earth. Stop reading for a moment and contemplate what you just read because it is completely true and mind-boggling.

Our scientists in astronomy, astrophysics, chemistry and many other deep scientific disciplines have been studying the universe for hundreds of years. These sciences include rocketry, the advanced engineering required to design a rocket engine, communications systems, metallurgy, chemistry to produce propellants, guidance systems that withstand huge amounts of vibration during the launch phase of rockets, communications systems, quantum mechanics, computer systems that are lightning fast to guide our satellites and rockets for the payloads we put into orbit.

Sophisticated optics for our telescopes, sophisticated accurate prisms that break up the incoming photons from planetary objects so we can measure the chemicals present, material science to choose the proper elements necessary to construct telescopes, rocket engines, radar systems, and the list goes on and on. This and so much more is required to make magnificent advances in our understanding of God's physical creation. It is a magnificent achievement for us to have accomplished sufficient objective scientific knowledge that we may be able to examine the cosmos to confirm that it is impossible for the cosmos to form itself out of nothingness. It must have an infinitely powerful and intelligent Creator to exist the way it does.

Very recently in human history, about 20 to 30 years ago, science began understanding how God designed and crafted this physical universe. All these scientific disciplines and many more were necessary to produce our current understanding of what God did so we can live on earth and make our grand decision whether or not to say yes to God and live with Him and the Trinity for eternity in paradise.

This scientific discovery also depends on a vibrant society that can produce the money for this costly endeavor and educate all the people in the sciences. None of this could happen without a literate society that has the motivation to look up into the sky and wonder where all that comes from and have the motivation to explore it in a scientific way. Almighty God put that wonderment into their hearts to explore the unknown, which is exploring the will of Almighty God when you think about it. To simplify things, let's look at two major areas.

In this section, I will discuss the proof that God did create the entire universe as we know and love it today. This universe is fine-tuned to unbelievably precise measurements that must be that way, or the universe will either not exist at all or will never be able to support human life for God's children to make their decision on Heaven or hell.

In the following section, I will examine the thousands of magnificently intertwined biological processes inside our bodies that must all work together to support human life. The biology of a human being is an incomprehensible number of irreducibly complex series of biological functions. I discussed irreducible complexity in the previous section.

That applies immensely to our bodies as well.

THE TWO MAJOR SECTIONS OF SCIENCE

These two major sections of science are:

1. The finely tuned physical cosmos.
2. The exquisitely fine-tuned biological science of our bodies

We will explore both of the above next. This proves beyond any doubt that our Heavenly and loving Father in Heaven did design both the cosmos and our bodies to work together. They work together in such a manner that it gives us his sacred children the opportunity to be redeemed from the sin that we inherited from our parents' sin and what we call the garden of Eden so long ago.

Remember, humans have two major parts, our mind/spirit and physical body. We live in the physical realm and the spiritual realm both at the same time. We already know that God sent us his only begotten son, that whoever believes in Him shall not perish but have everlasting life. (John 7:6) All we need to do as Almighty God's sacred children is to accept our Father's love for us and open our arms to Him, and He will accept us into his Heavenly Kingdom. He has created everything we see outside at night, so we can constantly be reminded of his eternal love for every one of his sacred children.

This means you and me and everyone else. 99.9% of the people on this earth have absolutely no idea what our Heavenly Father has done to create a path of redemption for them back to Him by creating both the spiritual and physical realms we live in.

So, God created the physical realm, and our scientists have given us so much understanding about how it works through wonderfully complex and fine scientific instruments and understandings. Many books have been written on this topic, and I will not bore you with all the details here, but I will give you a taste of what the science tells us these days. Dr. Hugh Ross has written several books, along with others, that explain in phenomenal detail how recent science has proven beyond a doubt that an infinitely powerful and loving Creator has indeed designed the entire universe.

THE CREATION OF THE PHYSICAL UNIVERSE

As hard as it may seem for us to believe, we were thought into existence in the blink of an eye by our Heavenly Father. Now, remember that Almighty God lives in many different time dimensions simultaneously. The Bible describes one day in Heaven as a thousand years on earth. We can only imagine what time must translate like in the other dimensions that Almighty God occupies.

But from our perspective in our universe, our physical universe began approximately 13.8 billion years ago from a very hot point of something beyond plasma and began expanding faster than what we call the speed of light. Astrophysicists call this the period of inflation. Recently the James Webb Space Telescope has uncovered anomalies in space that seem to contradict the "big bang" theory of how the universe started. Good. We are making more progress in understanding what Almighty God did for us. Scientists today have an enormously complete understanding of our universe back until the universe was only 10 X-43rd seconds old.

There is an exciting statistic about the first moment of physical creation. Max Plank, the renowned physicist, calculated that the temperature of the tiny sphere from which everything physical came from was 1.416 x 10 to the 32nd power. According to science, that is the maximum temperature possible in any physical structure. You should remember this number because it also means that time began when the universe began. In the book "The Creator and The Cosmos" by Dr. Hugh Ross Ph. D., He wrote, "of all the Holy books of the religions of the world, only the Bible unambiguously states that time is finite, that time has a beginning, that God created time, that God is capable of cause and effect operations before the time dimension of the universe existed, and that God did cause many effects before the time component of our universe existed."

After a time, our physical universe continued to increase in size and cool down from enormous temperatures, and atoms and then molecules started to form. Then according to the laws of chemistry, molecules and then more complex molecules began to form. Then far more complex minerals started to form. And then, because of the laws of gravity, enormous bodies of matter started to form, and because these large bodies of matter and velocity to them they began to spin around each other some of these large bodies of matter became so large that they compressed. Their insides got so hot that they triggered nuclear reactions and started to give off enormous amounts of heat, and today we call those stars. Huge areas of the cosmos became homes of millions and millions of stars which we now call galaxies. The lifetimes of the stars stretch into billions of years.

You would think this process of forming stars and then forming galaxies would be quite random, but you would be wrong. Early in this process, because of quantum fluctuations, you would find that it was far more a clumpy sort of arrangement where globs of stars would attract each other and leave large holes here and there, or there would hardly be any stars and subsequent galaxies. Over more periods of time, something very strange occurred that our scientists are puzzled about today, which is the appearance of what is called dark energy and dark matter. Scientists do not understand what it is.

We know it is there, but we cannot measure it directly but only by its effect on the matter that we can see.

SCIENTIFIC PARAMETERS THAT MUST BE TO SUPPORT LIFE ON EARTH

Referring again to the book by Dr. Hugh Ross, Ph.D. ***The Creator and the Cosmos***, he says the following parameters of a planet and galaxy must have values following within for life of any kind to exist. Then he describes 32 different parameters that are tightly bound for any life to occur on a planet in our universe.

From an exhaustive study using advanced statistics and the number of galaxies and stars in our universe, Dr. Ross concludes the following: With considerable certainty, we can conclude that much fewer than a trillionth of a trillionth of a percent of all stars could possess a planet capable of sustaining advanced life without divine intervention, considering that the observable universe contains less than a trillion galaxies, each averaging 100 billion stars.

By natural processes alone, we can see that no one planet would be expected to possess the necessary conditions to sustain life. In other words, dear reader, life in our galaxy is impossible, nor any other galaxy in our universe. It takes a divine Creator of enormous power and design to create a place within our universe to sustain life as we know it on our planet today.

Looking further at the data, we can judge that it is not even close. As a final note regarding our universe, we need to include the more recently discovered area of dark energy and dark matter. Dark energy is a repulsive force driving the continual expansion of our universe to the point where galaxies farthest away from us are receding faster than the speed of light, violating our known physics. Dark matter, which we cannot understand, is responsible for binding our galaxies together so that the outer parts of our galaxies spin far tighter to their new physics than they normally should be able to.

There are no explanations for these phenomena that we are observing. In one of the galaxies, we see across this universe, things should be flying apart. In the other case, the universe is indeed flying apart with no end in sight.

Earlier in this book, I talked about entropy and that hell is really entropy running wild, which is what we see on the outskirts of our physical universe. As we speak, we are seeing fewer and fewer stars as they disappear into the distance. If this continues, our visible universe will become smaller and smaller and smaller to the point where it will be only the earth that we see, and then our earth will dissolve as well into nothingness.

But for those who believe in our Father Almighty, we will be in timeless eternity with infinite fulfillment with our Father in Heaven, and the physicality of the universe will in no way affect us at all.

Our Blessed Earth. Home To God's Sacred Children
After that discussion about the creation of a place within a universe that will support human life, we now need to address the question of biology, which is the home of our bodies that contain two major parts. The first part is the physical part that must operate successfully within the physical realm described above. The second part is the spiritual part which is connected to the spiritual realm so we may connect to our beloved Almighty Father in Heaven. This is our very complex brains. If you think

our bodies can't evolve out of primordial sludge in a swamp somewhere, YOU ARE PRECISELY CORRECT!

For life to be supported in the universe by random chance is completely preposterous. Darwin was a good scientist for his time but very limited in the scope of what he had to say. Frankly, his ideas were picked up by people who wanted to extrapolate them a thousand times farther than he intended and use his limited theory to destroy the concept of Almighty God for their own political reasons.

It is only the purposeful ignorant communist/socialist left that wants to promote the hyper-distorted Darwinian evolution theory. Even Darwin said that if it can be shown that life did not proceed by small increments over large amounts of time, then his theory is wrong. And so it has been proven.

Nonetheless, I will show you the great intricate complexity of our bodies that Almighty God has created for us. All of this has been done for us, his sacred children, so we may choose to live with Him in Heaven for all eternity in paradise, described earlier in this book.

Through a rigorous analysis by the smartest people in all the different sciences that you'll find that it is doubly impossible for life to exist with the requirements for the human body to exist the way it currently does without a loving Creator and designer.

So, to summarize, God has created this physical realm that we live in so that we can accomplish our redemption from sin and give us the opportunity to go to Heaven where we will be able to live with our Almighty loving Father for all eternity.

Remember these key points:

1. This physical realm allows all things physical to interact directly with the spiritual realm. This interaction occurs within our minds and is acted out with our physical bodies.

2. What we do within the physical produces certain results. These results give us feedback as to what value systems and other characteristics are in our minds and, most importantly, within our spirits.

3. The smart person will use this physical realm feedback to change what is contained within their minds and spiritual being. In this way, we can consciously move closer and closer to Almighty God and his divine will for us.

4. Without the physical realm, we would not be able to change and would not be able to overcome our sinful nature. This is an extremely important point. The physical realm is constructed in such a way that it reflects the laws of our loving Almighty Father. All his other sacred children including yourself have an inborn fundamental sense of equilibrium and fairness.

   This is fundamental to every creation our loving Father has done. Living on this physical earth with other sacred children gives us the perfect opportunity to get feedback to our spirits so that we may choose to change our behaviors in our beliefs to be more in line with and consistent with the will and laws of Almighty God.

Also, it is only within the physical realm that God can meet us one-on-one and forgive us our sins so that we may ultimately join Him in the second creation and live in eternity with Him.

In this important section of this Biblical literature, I will now address in detail how there is complete agreement between science and Christian theology. Yes, I said that correctly. Most people have unthinkingly accepted the false assertion that there is God on the one hand and there is science on the other, and the two don't mix. <u>This is simply not true</u>. If we as children of God accept that God did indeed create all that is seen and unseen, as Biblical Christian theology says, then we need to accept that it was God and only God that created the entire universe.

As described in other sections of this work, all of God's creation exists to provide a pathway for his sacred children to return to Him in the Kingdom of Heaven. Remember, dear reader, that you and I are created sacred children of Almighty God. Our birth happened "in a blink of an eye." This is described elsewhere herein. Yes, you and I both lived with our Heavenly Father in the Kingdom for uncounted eons of time. This is partly why our Father knows each of us individually and in complete detail.

Regarding science, the fact is that our Father created all that is seen and unseen. Very Biblical. This directly means that God also created all of science. For what is science? It is the study of God's creation. It is impossible for science to investigate anything else other than creation itself. We are part of that creation. This demonstrates that our Father created every law of physical existence. He created all the laws of physics, Newtonian physics that we use for spaceflight, the laws of chemistry, all that is studied in astronomy, astrophysics, quantum physics, and particle physics studied in our particle accelerators like the one at CERN, which borders France and Switzerland, all disciplines of biology and a whole host of other scientific disciplines that study the work of Almighty God.

So, remember, 100% of all science is the study and discovery of scientific laws that our Heavenly Father created. They did not create themselves like a few harebrained professors like to preach. If there is a division between science and Christian theology, that only exists within the imperfect, ignorant, and demented minds of mankind and their lack of understanding of the true nature of creation.

OUR MAGNIFICENT PHYSICAL UNIVERSE

I admire those scientists who continually probe into the frontier of knowledge to deepen our understanding of God's physical creation. God has designed us with inquisitive minds who want to learn something new. Sadly, however, this may exclude the last two generations that show mostly no sign of intelligence. Sorry, perhaps that's a political comment. But the observation is true. There is a wonderful history of mankind's exploration and increasing understanding of what God created for us as part of his plan for our salvation.

We can begin our search for truth in India. Between the 15th and 12th centuries BC, the Hindu Rigveda thought the universe was a "Cosmic

Egg." It describes a cyclical or oscillating universe in which the egg expands and collapses in a cycle.

In the fifth century BC, Greek philosopher Anaxagoras said the cosmos was a primordial mixture that was set into a whirling motion by the action of "nous" or mind resulting in the different objects we see today. For this he was executed.

Later in the fifth century BC, Leucippus and Democritus said the universe was composed of very small indivisible, and indestructible building blocks known as atoms. Everything in the cosmos was built using different combinations of these atoms.

Aristotle said the universe was fixed in size with the earth as its center. The elements were fire, air, earth, and water.

These are just a few of the very early thoughts of intelligent people trying to understand God's creation as best they could. These men could not possibly know that all creation was beyond the universe and was created by God for our eternal salvation. God loves us, his sacred children, so much that He thought into existence the physical realm, the spiritual realm, sectioned off a part of that which is a prison for those going to hell.

MODERN-DAY SCIENTIFIC KNOWLEDGE TIGHTLY LINKS CREATION AND SCIENCE TOGETHER

Mankind has always yearned to understand everything that surrounds him. This is a fundamental curiosity embedded in us by Almighty God when He created us. God wants us to grow closer to Him so that we may understand the magnificence of God's power and his love for us. God wants us to understand Him through knowledge which leads to us loving Him.

This yearning for knowledge of God and his creation is insatiable because the more we learn, the more questions we have from our new knowledge. This is a virtuous and Holy cycle that gives God great pleasure. Through the dedicated efforts of many scientists throughout the ages, mankind has come to learn fantastic amounts of knowledge regarding God's physical creation and the characteristics of our spiritual nature. For now, I will stick to the physical side of things in this section.

For many centuries especially in recent history, the belief that science was completely separate from God. God was up there in the clouds somewhere. Our physical reality has nothing to do with Christian theology or any other religion. This was the prevailing view until recently because of the scientific advances we have established over the last 30 to 40 years. The problem is, from a political point of view, it is very convenient for so inclined politicians on the liberal side of things to continue this outdated and completely wrong philosophy of existence.

It is the liberal God haters that promote this crap. I will be kind and say they are willfully ignorant. They dare not update their scientific knowledge, which will result in the destruction of their fundamental value system. Today through the excellent scientific advances throughout all scientific disciplines, we have come to a critical point in the totality of our understanding of the universe and ourselves. We are now at the point for the last 30 years or so where our scientific instruments can detect details of our universe that confirm in a very objective manner the contents of Biblical scripture.

What has been written in the Bible regarding God's physical creation of our universe has been confirmed by scientific inquiry time and time again. This discovery from science has been derived by many of our most intelligent people on earth. What a magnificent discovery this is, for it aligns our thinking scientifically and philosophically toward a point where it confirms the existence of Almighty God and his creations, including us as his sacred children. At this point, we see more and more the homogeneous nature and connections between the physical and spiritual realms. Many books are written on this topic, and I will list them elsewhere in this book.

Although this book is not intended to address the details of God's sacred children, studies show that we children were made perfectly. The reason that all of us have health issues is due directly to Lucifer's rebellion and then the fall of Adam and Eve. We are now stained with sin.

THE BASIS OF SCIENTIFIC INVESTIGATION AND DISCOVERY:

1. Within human thought these days, ontological assumptions propel scientific investigation. In other words, what do we believe to be true about the underlying basis of existence? With that in mind, some of the scientific assumptions support modern scientific investigation.

2. The physical world obeys a kind of reasoning that is separate from human thinking.

3. The world is composed of physical objects that have different natures or attributes in physical reality, whether or not a human being is observing it.

4. The physical realm is the manifestation of pure thought. This can only mean Almighty God, for He thought into existence everything that is seen and unseen, which includes the creation of us, his sacred children made in his image.

5. An objective and coherent physical and spiritual reality independent of human thought.

6. Our world consists of an objective reality and the potentials that stem from it.

7. The first law of thermodynamics proves the necessary existence of God. [11]

8. There are more fundamental assumptions, but you get the idea. This is what underlies all scientific investigation.

THE OBJECTIVE SCIENTIFIC DATA

With all the above in mind, there are many scientific investigations and subsequent conclusions by independent scientists in multiple disciplines that all point toward an infinite Creator that designed all that is seen and unseen. Nothing happened by chance or coincidence. NOTHING!

The following is taken from a book written by Dr. Hugh Ross and his colleagues. I strongly recommend that you buy his book titled *The*

---

[11] https://www.secretsunlocked.org/science/science-proves-the-existence-of-Godcrets Unlocked -

Creator and the Cosmos. Many scientists from many different disciplines have contributed as well.

EVIDENCE FOR THE FINE TUNING OF THE UNIVERSE:

The universe did not just grow in a random patchwork fashion. No, it was intricately designed with different parts that have been fantastically fine-tuned to tolerances that we can barely imagine. Consider the universe like a fine Swiss watch of the highest caliber. There are many different parts inside Swiss watches, all of which must fit with marvelous precision. All these parts are interlinked with many millions of times better tolerances than the finest Swiss watch. All of this precision and fine tolerances have the goal of telling time. All the fine tolerances designed into the huge numbers of different parts of our universe are there with the goal of providing God's sacred children a place to live, giving us an opportunity to enter the gates of Heaven.

A FEW EXAMPLES OF CREATION'S FINE-TUNING

There are 35 separate investigations by many different scientists. All of these scientific investigations address a different angle or phenomenon of our universe. Here is a small sample to give you an idea of the magnificent scientific work done by so many different people that are necessary for our universe to exist the way it does to support life.

1. The expansion rate of the universe. If too fast, then no galaxies. If too small then the universe would collapse.

2. The strong nuclear force. If 2% weaker or 3% stronger, then life would be impossible anywhere in the universe.

3. The gravitational force. If stronger, then stars would burn out far too quickly to allow life. If two weak stars would never become hot enough to ignite nuclear fusion, that produces all the heavy elements required for our bodies to function.

4. The electromagnetic force constant. If 4% weaker or 4% larger, life would be impossible.

5. If neutrons were 0.1% more massive, they would not be enough to form heavy elements needed for physical life.

6. The total number of protons and neutrons in the universe must be exactly equal to an accuracy of one part in 10 to the 37th power. If not, then electromagnetism would be gravity, and there would be no stars or galaxies, therefore, no life in the universe.

7. The cosmic mass density must be fine-tuned to less than one part in 10 to the 60th power, and the space energy density must be better than one part in 10 to the 120th power. These fine-tuned requirements for life to exist within this universe go beyond human understanding.

8. The balance between dark energy and dark matter must be within something like one part in 10 to the 60th power. Elsewise, either the universe would expand so fast no chance for galaxy formation, or too slow, and everything would collapse in on itself.

9. There are 28 more scientific relationships that must be within very fine tolerances for life to exist on planet earth. The above is only eight. The conclusion here is that it is impossible for these tight dimensions to happen all by themselves. It must take an infinitely intelligent Creator that designed our universe. This is completely consistent with all Biblical literature. God is perfect, and his creations are perfect too.

NECESSARY GALACTIC RELATIONSHIPS FOR LIFE TO EXIST

The above is just for the universe to exist. There are many more variables that must be within an extremely narrow range for life of any kind to exist on earth. I will not take up any more space describing the myriad of relationships that must occur for the universe to exist as it does and for the earth to exist so it can support human life. All these are listed in detail in the book from Dr. Hugh Ross, "The Creator And The Cosmos."

There are 66 fine-tuned environmental requirements for many different relationships within our galaxy and our solar system that must be precise and exact in relationship to each other. If this does not happen, then life on earth will not exist even though the universe may exist.

FACTORS THAT DETERMINE THE PROBABILITY FOR ATTAINING LIFE SUPPORT ON OUR PLANET

The fact of the matter is that the probability for attaining life support on earth is 100% in reality. And the reason for this is because the Trinity was designing everything to fine tolerances so there was no chance that it would not work successfully. Probability is what only comes into the picture if chance was involved and there was no chance that anything would fail.

There are 128 different parameters that must fall in a very narrow range for each of these parameters as a probability factor that the parameter will be within that range as determined by our scientific community. The net probability that all this can happen by accident is zero. Of this, there is no doubt.

More accurately, it is one chance in 10 to the 166th power. There are not that many atoms in the universe to give you an idea of the chances that there is not a Creator. Said again, the chances are zero from a scientific viewpoint that there is no Creator. Our universe was designed and so to our local requirements that allow our earth to be able to support life.

In summary, the only explanation for the existence of our universe, the existence of our Milky Way galaxy, and the existence of our planet called earth that can sustain human life for a long enough period of time is Almighty God, our loving Father in Heaven is the Creator of everything that we see. Add to that the probability that our human bodies assembled themselves by random chance, is again at least as remote as the universe existing and supporting human life made in the image of God.

If you think the universe and the galaxy are impossible, the complexity of the human body goes far beyond that. The random chance that our bodies assembled themselves over the time available since the creation of earth is one part in 10 to infinity. Evolutionists should hang their heads in shame, and so to the political monstrosity called the Democrat party, a.k.a. liberals.

They use the ridiculous and discredited theory of evolution as their only way to deny Almighty God. Boy, what will they say when they meet Jesus Christ after they die? I would like to be there, hee hee hee.

There is no way at all that the universe, our galaxy, our planet Earth, and our human bodies were not created by our loving Almighty Father in Heaven. It is completely insane and ridiculous to even suggest such a monstrously stupid idea.

19

God Creates the Human Body

ENTER OUR PRECIOUS HUMAN BODIES

To put things in perspective, we have covered two of the three major creations our Heavenly Father has done for us, his sacred children. This is the spiritual realm and the physical realm known as our universe. Lastly, we will now cover our biological human bodies, which are miracles in and of themselves. Our Heavenly Father went to great lengths to provide us with the necessary pathway back to Him in the Heavenly Kingdom.

All we have to do is say yes to God and live by what Jesus Christ has laid down for us during our short lives on earth. It is by the way we behave on earth that determines our choice of either God or Satan. This has already been discussed. Now, onto our physical, biological bodies.

If you think that it is impossible for our bodies to randomly evolve by chance out of primordial sludge in a swamp somewhere, YOU ARE PRECISELY CORRECT! For life to be supported in the universe by random chance is also completely preposterous. For our bodies to develop out of a patch of fungus somewhere in a swamp is also preposterous. Darwin was a good scientist/botanist for his time but very limited in the scope of what he had to say. The more you know the facts, the more you will laugh at professors promoting the religion of human evolution and the universe. Remember that the theory of evolution has so many holes in it that it should be characterized as a second-rate religion.

Enter modern Marxist socialist politics in our country. Frankly, Darwin's ideas were picked up by people who wanted to extrapolate his theories to pathetic extremes and then expand his limited theory into political hyperspace so as to attack Christian theology. I call it the "Buzz Light Year" hypothesis, "to infinity and beyond!!" Political evolution's sole purpose is to mislead the masses and divert them from believing in the one true God that created everything. It's only the purposefully ignorant and the communist/socialist left that wants to promote the hyper-distorted Darwinian evolution theory.

Even Darwin would completely disagree with the perverted mess of today regarding his biological theory. Darwin said that if it can be shown that life did not proceed by small increments over large amounts of time, then his theory is wrong. And so, it has been proven that life did not evolve that way. Archeology has shown that life comes in spurts with no interstitial life forms. It jumps from one to a very advanced next one. Nonetheless, I will show you the intricate, irreducible complexities of our bodies that Almighty God has created for us. All of this has been created for just us. Why? So that his sacred children may choose to live with Him in Heaven for all eternity, in paradise described earlier in this book and our beloved Biblical texts.

And it is through a rigorous analysis by the smartest people in all the different sciences that it is doubly impossible for life to exist with the requirements for the human body to exist the way it currently does without a loving Creator and designer.

So, to summarize, God has created this physical realm that we live in order to accomplish our redemption from sin and give us the opportunity to go to Heaven, where we will be able to live with our Almighty loving Father for all eternity. Just think, dear one, we will never grow old in Heaven.

Our Body's Parallel Physical Complexity

At the organ level, biologists find an enormous amount of interlocking complexity needed to support life. It is with the same irreducible complexity and mind-boggling precision that is also necessary for our created human bodies to function and support our physical existence and spiritual connections. The amount of irreducible complex relationships

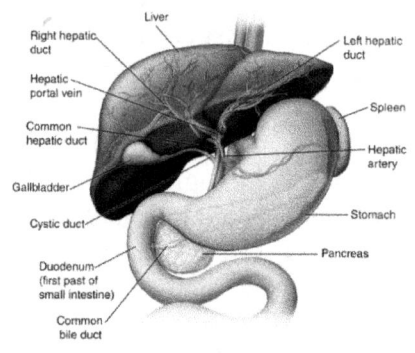

within our bodies is in the many multiples of thousands. There is not one part of our physical bodies that is not deeply involved in irreducibly complex relationships with other parts of our bodies. There is absolutely zero chance that our bodies happened through random chance with evolutionary development.

Our livers, for example, carry on more than 500 interrelated chemical processes that help support our lives. No one can live without a liver. It is even so central to our existence that it is the only organ within us that can regenerate itself after damage. Look at the picture above. Evolutionists say that all you see there happened by random chance selection—a role of the dice. Now multiply the above to all the rest of your bodily organs.

Does anyone honestly think this happened by random chance selection over a long period? If random chance is the driving force behind the generation of life on earth, then Las Vegas must be the fountain of youth and everything seen and unseen. Ridiculous, isn't it? It must be the casinos in the world that created you and me. However, the popular slogan remains "what happens in Vegas remains in Vegas."

If so, what is the guiding force behind all the dice rolling that resulted in a coherent liver? How many trillions of dice rolls did it take for 500 different chemical processes within our liver to reach the point where it supports human life? Remember, all of this is just for ONE organ. There are many others.

https://www.hopkinsmedicine.org/health/conditions-and-diseases/liver-anatomy-and-functions[12]

Consider our eyeballs. That is a magnificent example of exquisite design for an organic camera that feeds image-like information to a certain part of our brains so we can see. Otherwise, we all would be blind as a bat. The eyeball is an exquisite example of precise design and engineering to provide sight in all sorts of lighting conditions, from nighttime to stargazing to very bright light at the beach. To be able to see things close up for reading and far away for enjoying mountain landscapes. And our eyes do this all automatically without you thinking about it.

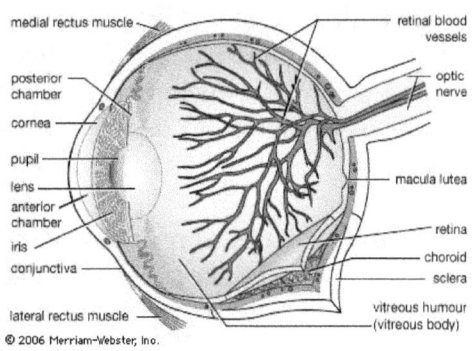

Do you really believe that random chances somehow produce our eyeballs over a long period of time? For me, that would be the height of ignorance and stupidity. Besides, how did our eyeballs connect to our brain through random chances?

The reason for the popularity of evolution in our Marxist leftist politics is because many people are stupid-ass ignorant! They just accept what someone in a position of authority says so. Remember, getting elected to some political position does not increase a person's IQ. If they were stupid and biased, to begin with, they will be stupid and biased in office. Terrible mistake! Our upcoming generations have never been taught in school how to think for themselves. Why? Because it is easier for a predatory socialist government to control stupid people than a society with intelligent thinking capability to reject idiot policies and use common sense.

A stupid society let Joe Biden destroy our energy industry such that he made our country dependent on foreign sources of oil again. Before he

---

[12] Body Chemical Processes: https://www.hopkinsmedicine.org/health/conditions-and-diseases/liveranatomy-and-functions

came on the scene, Trump made our country completely independent for our energy needs, with no foreign oil. The United States became a profit-making oil exporter for the financial benefit of our citizens. Biden consciously ruined our nation's security by what he did. An intelligent society would NEVER let that happen. There are evil forces at work within high government positions that aim to destroy the United States of America and its freedoms that reflect the will of God. Remember, God gave us free will, which means freedom to choose. The Democrat party continues to attempt to destroy this and from its nose at our Heavenly Father.

Accepting evolution shows how ignorant we have become as a country, and the list continues. Lastly, take this small liver example and extrapolate that to all the other bodily functions, and you will reject evolution completely. Just THINK, dear people. Use the brain God gave you and think for yourself.

In his book "*Improbable Planet*," Dr. Hugh Ross, Ph. D., says that design is the only way for our human bodies to exist, for all the connected biological functions. The sad news is that if left to normal random natural forces, "the probability for life's origin by natural processes alone "it may prove as low as zero."

Some statistics:

79 organs in our body that comprise 11 different organ systems with 206 bones must work together in flawless fashion.

https://www.britannica.com/science/aqueous-humor

Improbable Planet, Dr. Hugh Ross, Astrophysicist, Baker Books, 2016

https://anatomy.app/blog/human-anatomy/

Questions for evolutionists:

1. How is it that our skin knew to develop to protect us from infections and fungus?
2. How is it that male and female genitalia knew of each other so that they would evolve perfectly to fit with each other for reproduction?
3. How is it that our bodies are very symmetrical? For example, their left hand is the mirror image of her right hand. How did blind random selection know how to do that? How did one hand inform the other hand to be a mirror image?
4. How is it that evolution by random chance selected two eyeballs spaced apart from each other in such a way they fit inside our heads and connect perfectly with a certain spot in our brains to produce stereoscopic vision?
5. How is it that our feet have so many bones designed perfectly to absorb constant pounding without falling apart?
6. How is it that females have breasts for feeding their young? How did random chance know that a female body would need to do this in the future? How is it they have a vagina and a womb to create children out of a single egg and sperm? How did female genitalia and reproductive organs know they would need to support a developing human being during pregnancy?

There are many more common-sense questions to ask people if they do not believe our Heavenly Father and the rest of the Trinity designed and created the human body. As you may have detected by my slight change in language, I do not have any patience for people that do not take their responsibility seriously to learn things to the point where they are not led by the nose to believe things generated by satanic political individuals.

THE CELLULAR LEVEL

Not only are our human bodies dependent on extremely close tolerances at the macro organ level, but it is also truer at the cellular level. At the cellular level, there exists a great series of biological activities that our biologists are still working to understand. Biologists today do not understand all the functions of DNA and RNA and the mechanism they use to govern biological processes in the human body.

Yet evolutionists tell us all these extremely complex processes happened by random chance. Anyone that believes that is a fool. An individual cell is truly the fundamental building block of our bodies. Each cell is a fantastically complex series of irreducibly complex chemical reactions that scientists still do not entirely understand. The cell is the fundamental factory that allows life to occur at the organ level and in our bodies.

At the cellular level, our chromosomes, RNA, and DNA are contained. See below to get a rough idea of information about our chromosomes and just how complex they are within themselves.

In other words, left to the normal laws of physics and the natural law that God put into place before He created matter that filled the physical universe that we occupy, the result be that no earth would form from natural forces. No human bodies would form either.

A Heavenly body, or what we call a planet, would be necessary to be designed and created by our Heavenly Father with purpose and forethought. Almighty God would need to think into existence a home for his sacred children to occupy a planet so they can work out their destiny using their free will with the bodies that Almighty God has already designed in the spiritual realm.

These physical bodies and their spiritual component will be born into this physical universe after Almighty God intervenes and creates a physical home for them that we now call earth. It is here that the history of mankind begins and ends. The story of mankind starts with two people we call Adam and Eve. And the story is interwoven with an angel named Lucifer who fell from Heaven and is now called Satan and became the

Prince of the earth working very hard to destroy all of God's children made in God's image.

HUMAN GENOME AND CHROMOSOMES

In each human genome, we have 23 chromosome pairs in each cell nuclei in humans. They can be divided into two types: autosomes (body chromosome(s)) and allomone (sex chromosome(s)). Certain genetic traits are linked to a person's sex and are passed on through the sex chromosomes. The autosomes contain the rest of the genetic hereditary information. All act in the same way during cell division.

Within our cellular structures, we have 21,000 gene pairs with 3,079,843,747 base pairs of genes inside our chromosomes. The number of DNA bases paired in the DNA rungs is over three billion, measuring over six feet in length. Imagine that there is a DNA spiral helix molecule six feet long inside each cell in your body.

I am not going to make you a molecular biologist here. But ponder for a moment just how hugely complex all this is inside just one cell in our bodies. This complexity demands that every component MUST be in concert with all the other associated pairs inside every cell.

https://www.sciencefocus.com/the-human-body/dna/[13]

Summary

There is no way that all this biological stuff could happen without the direct involvement of the Trinity. This is direct testimony to the infinite power of Almighty God. His power goes down to each molecule inside the cells of our bodies. God crafted each atom to form each nucleotide which forms each strand of DNA and so on. Also, remember that all this discussion about cells applies to all other forms of life on our planet. The level of complexity considering not only human bodies but all the other animals, plants, and so forth on earth goes well beyond the capability of the human mind to comprehend it all. This is direct testimony for the miraculous love our Heavenly Father has for each and every one of us, his sacred children.

---

[13] Complex molecular pairs inside every cell in concert with all other associated pairs in every cell
https://www.sciencefocus.com/the-human-body/dna/

Our loving Heavenly Father did all of this. Why? It is to give each one of us the necessary resources to decide if we want to go back to the Heavenly realm and spend eternity with God in an unlimited paradise.

If some of God's children reject his offer, they will choose Satan and hell, where they will ultimately cease to exist through runaway entropy and be dissolved back into nothingness from where they came.

20

Lucifer
The Threat Against God's Sacred Children

SATAN THROWN OUT OF HEAVEN

To review many things already discussed, our loving Heavenly Father knew well in advance that one of his high angels would rebel against Him. No surprise to God because He lives from the alpha to the omega at all times in all dimensions. Therefore, loving his 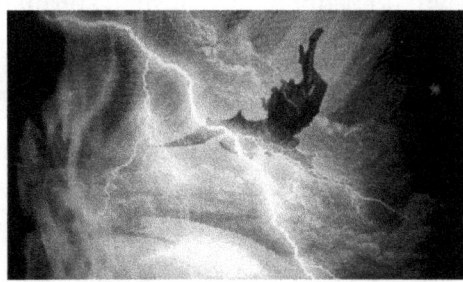 sacred children as He does, He prepared for the rebellion well in advance. He created the spiritual world. We are spiritual beings and will need that to communicate with our Heavenly Father. God already knew He would expel Lucifer and his angels of Heaven, so they needed a place to go. That's the other reason our Father created the spiritual realm. Also, God created a special place within the spiritual realm. It is called hell. Consider this a prison for all God's children who refuse and reject our Almighty Father. Our Father will not accept any form of sin into the Heavenly Kingdom. Heaven is a place of sinless love and devotion for all his children; likewise, his children will treat each other the same way. It truly is a perfect paradise. There is no stain of sin in the Heavenly Kingdom.

He also created the physical world we call the universe. This is to support our physical bodies so as to propagate all his children in order on the earth so they may test themselves as to where each child wants to go, either Heaven or hell. This is why you live on the earth today.

When Satan and one-third of the angels tried to rebel against our loving Heavenly Father, they were soundly defeated in the blink of an eye. And they were expelled instantly from the Heavenly Kingdom. They were driven down into the spiritual realm and onto the already existing earth. Satan was completely stripped of all standing in the Kingdom and became the prince of the earth. All this is described in the New Testament.

References:
I strongly suggest that everyone go to:
https://www.openbible.info/topics/satan_rebellion.

There you will see the many references in the Bible that discuss Satan. Every Christian needs to know this information. Because if we don't, we will do badly in the constant spiritual war that is being conducted against every Christian every day of the year. You may not think you are in spiritual warfare. If you think you are not, you are badly mistaken.

I am an active participant in this war, having been attacked hundreds of times throughout my life, starting with my parents when I was a little child. This is such an important topic for all Christians to realize and be educated in; I am seriously considering that my next book will be about Christian spiritual warfare against Satan. Many books are written on this topic, however, I feel they do not go deep enough and are not based on personal experience. My next book will include my personal experiences battling Satan and his demons.

It may seem odd, but after reading a book like this, you will come to love our Heavenly Father and the Holy Trinity far more than you do now. It is that much of a powerful topic. Revelation 12:7-12, NKJV, Isaiah 14:12, Luke 10:18, Revelation 12:4, Ezekiel 28:1-26

Your Life's Purpose in God's Grand Design

The Poem Of Evil

Satan Rebels and Attacks God's Children
But Satan saw and hated them down to his very core.
Our Father knew, before creation, hateful Satan makes horrible war.
Across all dimensions of time, he would try to destroy all he abhorred.
God's children became Satan's innocent target.
Clever and deceitful, his demons roamed finding those to annihilate.
Choose God or Satan, that is our choice always to make.
Our purpose in life here on earth. Learn to love or fall into hate.
Live your life as Jesus told, reject Satan and his deathly fate.
The first creation so very special indeed, built for sinners.
Oh yes dearest of sacred children, sinners just like you, just like me.
Our loving Father created a whole universe for all of us.
To pass his test, just love and accept his infinite glory.
Given a choice in this creation, to God the forgiven we will certainly go.
Or to Satan all unrepentant sinners will be condemned to flow.
On earth a planet fine-tuned for us,
a path to our Father spiritually grown.
These are the creations, meant only for us,
a path to God our eternal home.

God's Children Fall

*Darkness appears us unawares,
brace now comes life's fall from the Word,
No one spared, most caring not, banging drums only deadness is heard,
Crying for life's loving makes us converge, that me and thee now three,
But now choice does our union part, beehive swirling thy self-asunder,
Broken, woeful descent from realms hearing snarling from down under.
So, allow turn away on life's hurried flow, our destinies await us all.
Shot by sin, awful to see, live like lost souls, fallen that are ego ridden.
They make life and reality feel like a poisonous prison.
Ignorant progressives shout, blather, God is nothing, I will not listen.
"My body is mine; I will rid myself of that wretched thing within".
Shut up God! I want an abortion.*

*Kill the fetus I carry now, what horrific and painful, a sinful distortion.
Make murder legal across this land! Murder is only a delayed abortion.
Yet God said, "Thou shalt cancel not, for the murder contained within",
Satan laughs with a stenchful glee, shouts to all Gods kids come to me,
they rush to me now, kill God's kids kill them now, slithering cat meow!
especially the women with child or not, they're only a cow.
Remember! Sheep on the right the goats on the left. So, Jesus would tell.*

*Progressives admit themselves as on the left. Democrats don't care,
Lie their asses off, get the power and run with the money.
Do they know? They're going to hell? Pray for them us Christians do.
So, do they find God? Do very well? Avoid the terror of hell?
Destroyers of fabric life unstitched hurtful so, to sin they so very driven.
Believe progressive me and always me, is Satan's call!
Fun it is, do whatever I want, so I will "do it my way" so Sinatra sings.*

*Into wretched sin they will certainly fall. You and me, lets do a fling!
In contemptible sin they frolic with glee, give more money for me!
Caring not until they go, then the greatest shock, horrific blow.*

*They live no more and see Jesus Christ and loving Angels not around.
The atmosphere is not love ever so great, not ever so profound.
Explain all the pain and hurt they caused God's sacred children.
Cannot bear to see themselves through the lens of pure love.*

Your Life's Purpose in God's Grand Design

Ask Jesus Please forgive me now. Jesus responds with this,
*"**I never knew you, leave me now!**"*
After this moment so crushing and the final of finals,

Wailing and gnashing of teeth, screaming beyond anything heard
That is what is heard, the last of sinners that rejected our Loving Father
They arrived in hell, now they know.
All know not where they go, God who? They boast their feeble brains.
Smartest they think they are, but demons throw them painful flames.
So foolish and feign some that vision they are so tall.
Yet from Heaven so tiny and putridly so very small.
Fools know not they are fools,
Too stupid to know they are so very deluded.
This is what so loving God forgiven have concluded.
A permanent Luciferian prison and covered with putrid hell.
Rejecting the sacred call, return to your prison jail cell
"He is Risen", giving his life for all God's sacred children.
Those who love only themselves will not ascend,
They will remain in the first creation as nothingness awaits.

Reject Jesus Christ our Lord and Savior, hurt others,
And he will not affirm you too, because you hated.
Going to the realm of terrible sufferings that await.
To hell you will go and go to straight.

Those who do not acknowledge Jesus Christ, and follow his will,
They will go to the Hellish domain and dissolve apart into particles.
Go to complete nothingness with all it will not contain.
Everything will disassembled into particles, then nothing will remain.
*Ultimately all around you including "**you**" will be disassembled.*
Scattered particles next to nothingness, is all that will remain.

From nothingness you came and to nothingness you will go.
Not even a memory of your existence will remain,
For that would be something, so no, nothingness does not allow.
Those in the Kingdom might remember someone, but that memory
Will be gently and lovingly fade away like it never existed.

Your Life's Purpose in God's Grand Design

God's children rightly worry for our country today.
Sin abounds stinks stronger than ever before and in every way.
Orchestrated vile and lies does flood the air from broadcast news.
Hateful propaganda in America that God abhors, highest government.
Puts thousands in jail if they tell the truth.

Wretched sin now exists in the highest of government places.
Satan craves to destroy our land of freedom and liberty,
Cancel all God's divine graces, turn men into women,
turn women into men, let each other use the other's bathrooms.
Persecute those who love our Creator.
The devil is the universal freedom hater.
They want to remove our words of truth.
They crave to destroy real truth by calling them lies.
They want lies to prevail with their phony "ministry of truth".
This is obvious for those with eyes to see

Look with a loving heart, watch those from truth they flee.
Watch the evil contained, Satan's children, beastly they be
disintegrating they are for lies corrosive they exist
much like what Jesus did when he cursed the fig tree
beware of those with snakes for hearts

sadly so, leading our country to ruin, the Democrat party
good reason there is, their mascot of hate and gluttony
best mascot of all, Hillary sitting on a sway back donkey
Can we survive this Satanic onslaught?
Those in our media certainly hope it's not.
All the lies they tell, will surely send them all, yes all directly to hell.
Remember dearest Christian, Jesus will say "I never knew you!"

Will our Republic survive all these Satanic establishment shills?
I say resounding yes!
Our freedom God loving Republic can!
But it is not for free, to work and sweat we must go
Believe in God who established our country!
Follow his ways, his commandments, pray to him on one knee.
Satan, his children too, they will dissolve into nothingness
No more bother for us, in Christ we reside, and nothing less.

THE SPIRITUAL REALM IS WHERE SATAN AFFECTS GOD'S CHILDREN

There is a real danger for all people where Satan will use the power of spiritual things to deceive them for his evil purposes. Many people succumb to such things as sorcery, crystal balls, witchcraft, astrology, horoscopes, and magic. This usually happens to people with low IQs and in backward cultures and societies. It also happens with people that disregard the needs of others. Deep down, their spiritual nature is one of "me first and screw you." Unfortunately, we find many of these people in politics because they crave power over others. They never want to hear that Jesus Christ of the Holy Trinity came to earth to painfully sacrifice himself to form the final link between God's children and the Heavenly Kingdom. He came to serve, not to command. If you sincerely follow the example of our Lord and Savior, then you will do well in the eyes of Almighty God.

All of this "me first "spiritual value is so far away from the truth of loving Christianity. Also, this is pure treachery, and Satan can affect the human mind, provided the child of God allows this either consciously or unconsciously. It comes in the form of giving into lucrative temptation that looks good on the outside but kills the soul money inside. <u>Again, this is because our minds are directly connected to the spiritual realm where Satan plays his games with us sacred children.</u>

The good news is that I do have the spiritual power to get rid of them by commanding them to go back to hell, where they belong, in the name of our Lord and Savior, Jesus Christ. I use imagery of a huge flame thrower aimed at them, and away they go. Every Christian has the same power. Do not hesitate to use it. It is your Christian birthright. But all of this is such a distraction and nuisance that it is really irritating.

On another level, there are far more sophisticated ways that Satan tries to get to people. He can make something destructive look very attractive to people according to their personality and desires. In this way, he constructs temptations to lure people into sin. Whole books can be written on this topic, but I think you have the idea for now.

But do not fear Satan and his demons. He cannot force you to do something you do not want to do. He works by enticement and pleasure with sinful hidden hooks attached to whatever he offers. Always pray for God's protection and guidance in all things, and you will be just fine.

More on this battle with Satan in the following section about spiritual warfare.

21

What Happened in The Garden Of Eden

CREATION IS SPECIFICALLY DESIGNED FOR REDEMPTION

I have said this before, but it bears repeating. All of creation that is seen and unseen is for one specific purpose. All the realms God created are for the purpose of making possible our spiritual redemption from sin. He also created our magnificent human physical bodies for the same reason. I covered this in detail earlier, but it does bear repeating because it is so important.

If you are part of the physical universe, you are also in the universe's timeline. Your Father in Heaven selected this timeline in such a way that when his sacred children were born into the earth, they would have sufficient time to learn about the deepest parts of themselves, to learn about Almighty God from a different perspective, to understand that not only were they physical children but also, they had an extremely important spiritual side that could communicate with their Father and also respond. Remember that creation has two parts: the spiritual and physical realms. This is in addition to our physical bodies, which also have two parts. Both of these are designed in such a way that they match perfectly with the bodies of God's sacred children.

The physical part of our bodies serves to demonstrate our actions according to the spiritual part of ourselves. In this way, we can learn from the results of our actions. Our actions on earth have their origin in our spiritual selves, which include our minds. In this way, we learn about ourselves and our spiritual condition. This is so we can make changes if we are dissatisfied with what we have done. The physical world is basically a large feedback loop.

The whole purpose of the matching spiritual and physical realms is designed so that God's children can make a choice between our Almighty Father in Heaven or the rebellious Lucifer who was thrown out of Heaven. So, within the spiritual realm, there are competing forces in our free will to decide which destiny we choose. Either live in paradise for all eternity with our loving Father or choose Satan with his immoral and lawless ways that leads to ultimate extinction when entropy runs wild and dissolves the entire physical realm into nothingness.

A DEEP THEOLOGICAL QUESTION FOR A CHILD OF GOD

I would like you to ponder a very interesting deep theological question. It is certain that there will be vast amounts of God's children that will choose the path of Satan and hell. God's Holy and sacred children will be living with Him in the Trinity in the infinite Heavenly Kingdom for all eternity. My question for you is: Will we, God's children in the Kingdom, cease to remember those that we knew on earth and beforehand when those that reject our loving Almighty Father dissolve into nothingness? Will we remember those that chose Satan and leave behind no trace of their existence whatsoever? They have evaporated into nothingness. Will we remember them in some fashion? Or will it be as if they never existed at all? Think about this. It is a reality within all existence. Said a different way, does nothingness include no memory of the past?

I know the answer to this question, but I will withhold this from you. Beloved Lord and Savior Jesus Christ told me the answer and why the answer is what it is. This is one time that it is appropriate that you might, dear sacred child of God, profit greatly by deeply thinking about the answer to this question and why the answer must be what it is. Due to cosmic cycles the ability of earth to support human life will start to decrease quickly.

THE GARDEN OF EDEN

The earth is the result of 8.5 billion years of development from a singularity created by our Almighty Father. Previously our Father created all the rules and principles that will guide the manner in which this singularity will expand. All of this physical development will ultimately result in one singular planet that is intended to address the decision-making needs of God's sacred children. It is here on this planet we call earth that all of God's sacred children will be born.

This physical earth has been positioned within all of the universe in such a way that it will develop into the perfect physical environment for God's children to be born and fulfill their choice of their destiny. Great scientific books discuss this development in the most precise manner, demonstrating that God has perfectly designed all the factors of this universe so that the earth and its cycles of existence will indeed support his sacred children to decide what their destiny will be. It should be noted that these earthly cycles which support human life on earth are coming to an end. Scientifically speaking, detailed analysis indicates that the favorable environment on earth will be ending shortly. From there, it will be harder and harder to sustain human life on this planet.

A VERY SPECIAL PLACE, THE GARDEN OF EDEN

In addition to the earth and the universe being designed perfectly for his children, there was also a very special place on earth we call the Garden of Eden. It is here that the very first of God's children came into being. It was a perfect place for the first two of God's children to live in. It was a paradise where Adam was given the task of naming all of the animals that were already there to greet him. Eve arrived to support Adam in his activities and give him the companionship and love that he needed.

Now, the purpose of God's children being born on the earth was again, so they have the opportunity to choose the pathway back to our Father in Heaven. All of God's children were created eons before and lived with their Almighty Father in Heaven as spiritual beings. Now, because of the vicious rebellion of Lucifer against their Almighty Father in Heaven, all of the sacred children must decide with their free will if they are going to take the path back to their Father in Heaven or not.

This is why God put the tree of the knowledge of good and evil in the center of the Garden of Eden. Whatever they chose, that action would directly affect all their descendants. This is enormous. If Adam and Eve followed the singular command of God and NOT eat of the fruit from the tree of knowledge of good and evil, they would, and all of their descendants would remain on the pathway back to our Creator and loving

Almighty Father in Heaven. They would then start to enjoy eternity in paradise with their Father.

This paradise would have no end and no limitations upon all of his children. However, sadly they chose to eat from the tree of good and evil because Satan tricked them. He lied to Eve, and she then lied to Adam. This simple action that disobeyed their Father, Almighty God, now doomed all of their descendants into scratching the ground for their sustenance and survival. From now on, life would be very difficult. From then on, Satan will run rampant across the face of the earth, tempting and tricking all of God's children that were born unto the earth and descendants of both Adam and Eve. Now Satan has the golden opportunity to strike back at Almighty God for throwing him out of the Heavenly Kingdom and down into the spiritual realm, hell and on earth.

It was now that Satan would begin to gather up as many of God's sacred children as he could through all manner of deception, destruction, chaos, confusion, and every negative thought that exists.

QUESTION: HOW DOES THE IMPERFECT ARISE OUT OF THE PERFECT

How can it be that Adam and Eve could not see through the deception of Satan? It seems easy for us today to point out how wrong she was and wonder how she could choose so badly. Did not God give Adam and Eve sufficient intelligence and perception not allow this to happen? Remember also God is perfect in all ways. God created Eve. So, it can be said that perfection created Eve; therefore, she must be perfect. Eve's free will must have the capability of choosing perfectly. Then why did she stumble so badly and then follow that up by lying to Adam? Does not perfection beget perfection? What happened in reality?

I asked this question of our Lord and Savior, Jesus Christ. This is how He responded.

August 24, 2022, 3.17 PM
Jesus Christ

Ahh my dear son, you came up with a very good one this time. It is a conundrum within the sphere of logic. Eve had no ancestors so nothing imperfect could have been imparted to her by anyone else. It was only God that created Adam, first. And since Adam provided his hip for the creation of Eve, that still remains a process of perfection. Therefore, both Adam and Eve were perfect with their Godly gift of free will.

Therefore, you can accurately say that they were very naïve having been on earth for a very short period of time before Satan took advantage of them. Even though they looked like physically and somewhat mature human beings, they were not. They were like children from a spiritual and knowledge perspective. Therefore, it was easy for Satan to strike against Almighty God and fool his children into eating from the tree of the knowledge of good and evil. They just had no experience in deciding things like this.

After Eve ate the sinful fruit, she immediately changed from moral perfection into a sinner. She now knew what evil was and what evil could do. As is the case with sinners, they always want to cover-up their dirty deeds. Eve is no exception. So, she lied to Adam and told him untruths about the fruit and what it was.

Now! Did God allow Satan to destroy his plan? God did know ahead of time that this would happen. For again, your Father in Heaven lives in the future as well as the past and in the now. He exists outside of your dimension of time as I do as well. Therefore, in order to achieve his intention of testing his sacred children about if they want to live with Him in paradise or live with Satan and ultimate dissolution into nothingness, He had to allow this transgression to happen.

This was a choice of free will on the part of Eve. She could have chosen differently. If that was true, if she refused the fruit, all of salvation history would not have happened. This includes Jesus Christ's dying on the cross for the forgiveness of our sins. Everything would be completely different.

If this were the case, then all of God's sacred children would never know if they were truly deserving of their great place in the Heavenly Kingdom or not. They would not know if they would pass the test of providing proof to both themselves and all realms of existence that they indeed are deserving of living with their Almighty Father in paradise for all eternity. It would remain unknown for all eternity and that is not tolerable within the Heavenly realm.

Continuing on, we now see the continuation of Adam and Eve's struggle for survival after they were banished from the garden of Eden. This is the way the human race lives today. Every day is filled with work and other activities designed to produce the necessary goods and services that we need for our family's survival. It is now that each and every one of us is being given a choice. Either follow in the steps of our Lord and Savior Jesus Christ or do not live within the commandments and principles of what Almighty God has given us. We prove by our actions and work if we deserve to go back and live with our Almighty Father in the Heavenly realm or NOT. All that we experience today is the result of the decision of Eve ever so long ago.

Question: Is the story of Adam and Eve in the garden of Eden an actual event in human history, or is it instead a myth or metaphor for something that happened?

August 24, 2022, 3:40 PM

Again, another good question. Needless to say, there was no one around at the time to record anything that happened other than what is documented in the Bible by Christian prophets. They are an excellent source by the way of good and accurate information for Christians. But we must allow them some literary freedom on some factual matters so they may deliver us actual information about what Almighty God wants to communicate to us.

In the case of Adam and Eve in the Garden of Eden, this is an accurate metaphor that documents what happened. There really was two people, male and female, that were the first to inhabit the earth in a very lush setting that provided great quantities of food for their survival. Since they were the first of God's sacred spiritual children to be born into the physical, your Father in Heaven paid close attention to their activities on this earth. He was always available to them to answer their questions, to soothe their fears of which there were lots and so on. It was not easy for them to be in such a strange place in a different realm away from what they were in before. Even though they had their memories temporarily removed, there still were lingering urges about what it was like before they came to earth. This is true of the human mind in general. We still retain some thin reminders of the past even though we have forgotten.

Although this story is a metaphor, it is an accurate one and is not invented or made up in any way to produce something falsified for the benefit of the story in the Bible.

22

Inescapable Hell

HOW HELL FITS INTO GOD'S CREATION

Now here is something that I think no one ever thought of, linking the existence of hell inside the spiritual realm and it being part of God's plan for creation. Why does God allow Satan and his demons to exist and cause havoc on his children? There are good reasons to understand that Satan's time is growing short. As I said before, the increasing entropy we see in our universe today will dissemble everyone that rejects our Heavenly Father into a chaotic mess until they finally dissolve or evaporate into the nothingness from which they came.

WHY HELL STILL EXISTS

Hell is a place within the spiritual realm, the same spiritual realm connected to the physical realm (as we discussed before). To review, both the spiritual and physical realms were created specifically for God's children so they may choose to be with their Heavenly Father in paradise for all eternity. Remember that all of creation was designed and implemented so that God's sacred children have the opportunity, through their own free will to choose either their Heavenly Father or the ways of Satan. Without creation, God's children would have no opportunity to make this eternal choice. Creation is indeed a monumental act of love for his children.

For those of God's children that through living their lives on earth, reject our Heavenly Father, they will understand that they need to live out their existence in hell. Heaven is no longer a possibility for them due to their conduct on earth. God created hell so these children will have a place to go where they cannot interfere with all others of God's children as they work out their destinies as well. It is a prison. It reminds me of the "Roach Motel" that was advertised long ago. It was a trap for cockroaches. The advertising slogan was, "They can check in, but they can't check out."

Rarely for spiritual reasons agreed to by our Father, a few of our other sacred children are taken to hell by some of God's powerful angels. This is to show them that they better straighten up, or hell is their destiny. Look up on the internet their testimonies after they return to earth. They say it is ghastly and completely horrific beyond anyone's imagination. Many good websites have this kind of information provided by people who went to hell and now want to warn others about the horrors that await if they reject our loving Father.

Remember that Lucifer was cast down out of the Heavenly realm and into the spiritual realm that is connected with the physical realm, which includes the earth. Hell occupies a very small portion of the spiritual realm. I imagine it is somewhere in the boonies, far away from everything else. Remember that Jesus Christ said that the spiritual realm is enormous. It is a dreadful place that is a one-way street that children that go in never come back out. Hell is relatively small compared to the size of the general spiritual realm.

GOD'S CHILDREN AND HELL

Once a child, through their voluntary acts, decides to go with Satan, that person goes to hell and is confined there. There is no escape from hell for any of God's children that reject their Almighty Heavenly Father and instead choose the ways of Satan. There is one way in and no way out. These children have made their choice, and it is irreversible.

There is a sacred complete life review of that child. No detail is overlooked. That child is shown in detail why they will not be allowed into the Heavenly Kingdom. All of the reasons are based upon all aspects of a child's life on earth. This means all the sinful and evil choices of free will they did, their interior attitudes and emotions that led to evil behavior. They are also shown all the opportunities within their past life that they could have chosen the Godly way but rejected. They are held accountable for all the damage they have done to others of God's children. It is shown to them in great painful detail.

WHY CAN SATAN STILL ENTER HEAVEN?

Now, one may ask how is it then that Satan has access to the general spiritual realm and do his evil upon God's children who exist on earth.

Why can he still enter Heaven? The answer is both Satan and his demons remain angelic beings with all the power that comes with that. However, Satan and his demons still have the power of an angelic being. So, they may freely go from the place of hell into the spiritual realm or back again as they choose of their own free will.

On the other hand, God's children are not angels and do not have the same power. This means that God's children that reject their Heavenly Father have no escape from that place within the spiritual realm, we call hell. I want to emphasize that. Once a fallen child of God chooses the ways of Satan and physically dies, that child meets with God's sacred angels.

This is done very lovingly because remember that Heavenly angelic beings do not have an ounce of negativity, hatred, or anger within them. That is not in any way part of their nature. They are fountains of pure love, a true reflection of the deep and abiding love that is an immutable characteristic of our Heavenly Father. People who have chosen hell through their actions, thoughts, and other evil attributes quickly come to know where they chose evil; because of that, they will not be allowed into the Heavenly Kingdom. Books can be written about the edge cases like those who are truly mentally ill and other conditions where there is a mixture of evil chosen by a child of God and evil that comes from a sickness they have through no fault of their own. It boils down to whether or not they chose evil through their own free will.

GOD GIVES HIS CHILDREN EVERY POSSIBLE OPPORTUNITY TO ENTER HEAVEN

Some of God's marginal children are allowed into Heaven with loving care and support. They will squeak into Heaven by the skin of their teeth. Your Father in Heaven wants to give all his children every possible opportunity to spend eternity in paradise with Him. These marginal situations of God's children are sectioned off into a part of the Heavenly realm where they are ministered to in the ways they need to become full-fledged citizens of Heaven. Lord Jesus Christ reminded me of someone I knew closely now in hell

October 15, 2022
Jesus Christ

In one case my dear son that you personally know of and were involved in, the woman you knew was so mangled emotionally by her mother she could not overcome the destructive emotional attitudes and deep anger and rage that was generated by the treatment she received as a child. My dear son, I know that you worked so very hard to save this woman from herself. Then years later after you parted ways with her, she passed away and appeared to you multiple times.

You did not realize that she had died. You remember the moment when she appeared to you in utter terror and was screaming, "Help me Help me!" You remember that I then told you that you needed to help her and you told her to take my hand and I will lead her to Heaven. She did so and she entered into Heaven.

After that, she entered into Heavenly rehabilitation to recover from the damage her mother caused her and to understand the many times she created evil in the world. The rehabilitation included psychological healing for her, therapy for her negative emotions that were strong within her and education about what is needed to be a citizen of the Heavenly realm. Our Heavenly angelic beings did everything they could for her but through her free will she decided that all this was just too much for her and she ended up feeling very uncomfortable residing in Heaven. So, very surprising to you, she chose to live in hell where she thought she could be herself and do whatever evil she felt compelled to do.

This is one example of an edge case that even when a child of God is literally carried into Heaven, they still may choose hell instead because that is all they know and they actively reject living in paradise even after having been there. I know this is still hard for you, but you experienced it with me.

It is not that the power of Heaven is limited, rather in all cases like this your Heavenly Father will always honor the free will choices of all his children. In this case your dear friend used her free will choice to willingly enter into hell where she could have no rules to live by knowing that she will ultimately go back into nothingness from which she came.

I note this saddens you deeply my dear son. But your Father in Heaven will always honor the free will choices of his children. Just keep on doing the magnificent sacred things you continue doing for the benefit of God's sacred children.

Question: After a child of God enters into the Heavenly Kingdom is there any chance that somehow, they may fall out of Heaven and end up in hell? Our Lord and Savior Jesus Christ Continues:

September 15, 2022, 8:40 AM
Jesus Christ

It is true that it is not impossible for a child of God once in Heaven to resign so to speak and enter hell instead. However, this only happens to those of God's children who are allowed entry into the Kingdom on a probational basis. As I said earlier your Father in Heaven provides every opportunity possible to allow all his children to enter his Kingdom of Heaven. The earlier case of the woman that entered Heaven with your help, dear son, she was there on a probational basis subject to participating in all what was needed to erase the evil tendencies that remained within her. She chose to not complete her therapy and chose instead to enter hell. This was an eternal choice on her part. The same is true with others of God's children that are so very marginal they cannot be allowed into the full aspects of the Heavenly realm. There is part of Heaven that is separate for the very purpose of rehabilitating children who are forgiven but retain very strong evil tendencies. That will not be allowed into the Kingdom. They must work hard with the sacred beings that are there to help them achieve what is needed to enter into the full glory of Heaven.

For all of God's children that clearly decide through their free will they want to enter the Kingdom of God and remain there this certainly will happen. Each child of God however although completely forgiven of all their sins there still remains within them a slight tendency that leads to disunity. This is why, although it is never discussed within the Godly Christian community, each of God's children does go through a Holy purification process. After completing that there is no chance that they would ever entertain any thought of leaving the Kingdom or doing anything that would perpetrate that. In fact, anything outside of the infinite Heavenly Kingdom is never thought of. The idea of something called hell becomes a very distant historical note and nothing more.

In other words, they will retain their free will completely after entering into the Heavenly Kingdom. Their hearts are purified and it is such a lovely process that it brings such joy, such fulfillment and love into their hearts that any thought or any possibility of leaving God's eternal Kingdom vanishes completely. I wish that the Christian community, the Godly communities of the world would understand this better but for now it is really not discussed at all. I'm glad dear son that you brought this up. It helps complete what is intended by all creation provided by your Heavenly Father and other members of the Trinity including myself of course.

23

God Prepares Redemption

As an old antacid commercial used to say, "oh, what a relief it is." Our Lord and Savior, Jesus Christ, is finally in town. Let's face it, humanity was in a pagan mess, full of totally narcissistic self-important, mentally ill pagan kings along with sorcerers and witch doctors. Eking out a living meant paying bribes to all the local power structures not to bother you until the next time. Now born into the world is the final link, the crucial link that is needed between God's sacred children and our Heavenly Father to create a pathway for us to return to the Heavenly Kingdom from where all of us originally came from. Yes, my dear Christian friends, all of us, you and me, spent our first many eons of existence with our Heavenly Father in the Heavenly Kingdom before we came to earth. Lovely thought, isn't it? Better yet, if you love the rest of us, you will be going back for all eternity.

THE ROLE OF JESUS CHRIST

The role of Jesus of Nazareth was pivotal for the redemption of all of God's sacred children. Without Jesus of Nazareth becoming the Christ, there would be NO salvation. None! Before Jesus, the linkage between God and mankind was broken because of sin. That happened due to Adam and Eve eating from the tree of the knowledge of good and evil. In all of creation, Jesus Christ was absolutely necessary for the salvation of all mankind. Why is this?

Jesus Christ is both fully human in every respect and concurrently He is fully God. He is completely God in all manner of existence. Jesus is a member of the Trinity. It is Jesus that created all of creation. Our Heavenly Father felt that our Lord and Savior would be responsible for all activities related to the redemption of all of God's children.

There can be considered to be two major elements necessary for our redemption. The first is all creation itself. Our entire physical universe and multiple spiritual realms are necessary for they provide the fundamental spiritual pathway back to Heaven for all God's sacred children. Within the physical universe God's children have the opportunity to demonstrate their love for God. Or sadly, they can demonstrate their rejection of God and his rules and commandments. It is behavior of God's children that is determinative. All God's children will be judged by their actions in the physical universe, on earth. This judgment will be final for all eternity.

Simply put, God's children must show our loving Almighty Father, their acceptance of Jesus Christ, God's only begotten son, accept the Holy Spirit which proceeds to us. The second is of course our loving Lord and Savior Jesus Christ. It is He that is the necessary linkage between Heaven and earth. There is no other. I repeat, there is no other. Without our Lord and Savior Jesus Christ and what He did, there would be no chance for any of God's children to be redeemed for entry back into the Heavenly realm.

Remember, Jesus Christ is both fully human and fully divine. Jesus Christ came to this earth knowing that He must endure the sacrifice of death to wipe out the sinful state of all children of God. Jesus Christ wiped out the sin of Adam and Eve when they fell out of grace because of the lies of Satan in the Garden of Eden.

Also, Jesus Christ established his church so that it would continue to preach the gospel of our Lord forever into the future and until God sends his son back to earth for a second time. We do not know when that is, and nobody knows, not even our Lord Jesus.

MARK13:32 "But as for that day or hour no one knows it – neither the angels in heaven, nor the Son – except the Father.

"The precise moment of the Lord's return cannot be calculated by anyone. When the Lord spoke these words, that information was said to be known by only the Father. Christ was obviously speaking from the vantage of His human knowledge. (Luke 2:52)

The above is an oversimplification of our Lord and Savior's actions on earth for our salvation. Jesus Christ is ever so loving that He forgave the criminal next to Him on the cross and told that both of them would be in paradise before the day is out. This is a phenomenal thing that almost everybody ignores. This means that the very first child of God to enter the Heavenly Kingdom was a criminal. This speaks loudly about redemption and the forgiveness of sin if you accept God and his commandments and accept His only begotten son as our beloved Savior.

Only through our Lord and Savior, Jesus Christ, who is the way, the truth, and the life, are we allowed to go to the Father. There is no other way except by Him, Jesus Christ. Our Lord and Savior. Jesus Christ is the foundation of our church, our beloved Christian church. Why do you think that there is a cross in front of the altar at every church across the entire world. Every mass that is ever said celebrates His crucifixion without which there would be no salvation for mankind. Every human being on earth owes everything to our Lord and Savior Jesus Christ. Every person that reads this book owes everything to our Lord and Savior Jesus Christ. This is not an exaggeration.

Our Lord and Savior has a continual presence with each and every one of us throughout our lives. Yes, this is true for our Heavenly Father and the Holy Spirit which proceeds from our Holy Father and the Holy Spirit which proceeds from them. But it is our Lord and Savior that died for us that made it possible for us to return to the Heavenly realm from which we came. Remember, all of us at one time in the deep past all of us were spiritual children that enjoyed the Heavenly realm, the Heavenly endeavor with our Father and His Only Begotten Son and the Holy Spirit in the Heavenly Kingdom for eons before we came to earth.

It was our Father's only begotten Son that came to earth and died in excruciating death for us so that we may return to the Heavenly Kingdom and live eternity with the Trinity again. This makes Him ever so special in our hearts. I love my Heavenly Father ever so much and my love for my Heavenly Father runs deep beyond anything I can put into words. I love my Heavenly Holy Spirit just as much as it goes beyond words as well. But I love my Lord and my Savior beyond words and my love for Him is ever so close in my bond to Him. He is something of a brother that is a deepness and richness that is ever so close of a bond like that of the family member.

In many ways the role also of our Lord and Savior Jesus is the intercessor for us to our dearest Father in Heaven. It is our Father that loves us so very much and He is the final authority figure that makes the decisions for us with our ultimate well-being in mind. He is the one that makes sure that we stay on the proper path so that we do not hurt ourselves in any way for He knows what is best for us in all manner of being. He is the one that we can trust under all circumstances. And it is our Lord and Savior Jesus Christ that works with our Father to decide for us what is best and explain to us what we should do under all circumstances and works with us to obtain the actions we need to take as is appropriate. Both love us beyond anything we can possibly imagine. They along with the Holy Spirit, it is the Holy Spirit that comforts us in all manner of being.

So, we may boldly say: "The Lord is my helper. I will not fear. What can man do to me?" Hebrews 13:6 (NKJV)

Jesus Christ is the same yesterday, today, and forever.

This statement helps us look backward and forward so that we can know He is reliable today and that the things He has said are reliable (Hebrews 13:8). Believers can be encouraged that He will never forsake them or leave them (Hebrews 13:5). Believers should imitate the examples of those who have had faith in Him (Hebrews 13:6)

24

Who Really Is Jesus Christ In Our Lives?

Eons ago we were yet to be, you dear Lord, the Holy Spirit, our Father.
You all were in the heavenly Kingdom within the Trinity.
Your love for all things exceeded that existed beyond that we could see.
All your power and your love far exceeded that which was.
You existed with the Trinity into the future, you could see what will be.
And you saw all your children including me yet to be.

Thank you for that my dearest Lord. Humble as I am dedicated to thee.
Son of our Father, begotten not made, one in being with the Father,
Light from light, one in being with the Father,
through Him all things were made,
Light from light, true God from true God,
His song of love He shall serenade
To all God's Sacred children who he died for now in Heaven
It is true our Lord and Savior Jesus Christ knew before, we would sin.

Before Eve was tempted and fell, all earth was perfect and all was well.
It was the Kingdom of Heaven on Earth, no pain, delicious food, much
To do, busy tending the animals, all of them. Life was a free lunch.
Both ate the forbidden fruit everything changed, they felt condemned.
As well they should! Them brought to humanity immeasurable suffering.

From that point in the Garden of Eden, hardship and pain now begin
The Trinity knew ahead, God's plan for His children began to unfold.
Satan tempted Eve, she lied to Adam, he ate, now sin he couldn't elude.
Out of Eden into hardship and pain, work for your food,
Toil in the dirt, nothing now easy, that will never cease.
Now painful all generations to come, evil at every corner, lies increase.

Your Life's Purpose in God's Grand Design

The heart of Jesus breaks, Jesus cries for all his children,
he weeps for their pain, that shouldn't be, yet it is.
Pain and torment descends on the land to the babies as they cry.
The innocent in pain weep for reasons they know not why.

Foregone is the promise of eternal life on earth.
With the lies and treachery of Satan, that affects every human birth.
When Eve ceded to satan's lie and lied to Adam sin entered humanity.
The Heavenly Kingdom on earth and now the only begotten son Jesus,
will act to bring all God's children back into the Kingdom.
Back to our home.
And he shall by giving of Himself by His love.
To all people he said shalom

The pathway between those that accept their Father's love
for them and his ways it is the Heavenly realm. We are beloved!
It is these children of our Loving Father
that kept His ways and put others first,
Others were first with given love from Gods sacred Children.

25

Where Perfection Meets Sin

It is appropriate and necessary that we fully understand the intersection that occurs within our Lord and Savior, Jesus Christ—remembering that Jesus has yet to become the Christ. He has yet to become the pastoral lamb, the perfect sacrifice that must be paid for all the sins committed by mankind to wash away everything in atonement and full payment that all started with Adam and Eve so long ago. After this is accomplished, all children must be symbolically baptized to wash away their sins and then live a life of truth and honesty to the best of their ability, regularly confessing their sins to the church of Jesus Christ.

This is fundamental Christian teaching as established by our founding Fathers. But we must take a microscopic view of what took place within our Lord and Savior Jesus. For He was truly 100% God and 100% human. He was the only man that was this way. He was the only one that destroyed sin with Godly perfection in the moment in which our Lord and Savior uttered the words "It is Finished!" Jesus brought together both sin and Godly purity in one body we call Jesus Christ.

Inside our Lord Jesus, the two intermingled in such a way that it was God's love that triumphed in glory, for Satan tried every trick in the book to tempt Jesus away from his love for his Almighty Father in Heaven and all his sacred children. Nothing worked. Satan was doomed to fail from the very beginning.

Yet inside our lord and Savior, a battle must have raged on between the human side of Jesus and the other divine side of Him. One tugging against the other. What was that like, my Dear Lord?

November 17, 2022
Jesus Christ

My dear son you certainly do have a talent for asking very deep intellectual questions that are right on. In many ways one half of me was in constant battle with the other half. It was like banging both sides of a drum at the same time. The echoes of that got to be pretty nauseating frankly. The nausea of course came from my human side. But my divine love for everything was so intense that the painful part would soon dampen away and I would regain my footing. Quickly.

One problem I continually had was that I instantly gathered the reputation of being a healer. Everybody wanted me to heal them instantly. But the Trinity does not work that way. Healing means amplifying the natural bodily process of healing. Miracle healing amplifies natural healing process in the subject to the patient believing that they are being healed so it takes time. If healing was instantaneous, I would never get anything else done. Enough on that.

Back to the point of being divine and human at the same time, I always tried to keep my Father's message in simple agrarian terms. This was simply because everyone was in one way or another attached to farming. Everyone knew about farming and this would be an easy way to explain things to them. Inside of me there was no dividing line between divine and human. The human mind is not set up that way. The human brain is set up for there are modules of different functionalities where there is a site or one spot where there is hearing, in another spot there is cognition, in the third where there's quantitative skills, in another and so forth. So, it is not like putting one hand to the other where one is divine and the other is human. It is not at all like that. It is far more complex and deeper.

26

Our Blessed Mother Mary

AN ANGEL APPEARS

Our dear Mother Mary, what was life for you before the angel came to you and asked you if you were willing to become with child who would be the Savior of all mankind?

MARY SPEAKS ABOUT WHEN GOD'S ANGEL APPEARED TO HER

August 4, 2022
Blessed Mother Mary

Oh, my dear son Richard there was a tumultuous time in our lives as Hebrews. The Romans were constantly marching about from house to house making their presence known and looking for any criminals that might have been on their list. They were ever so intrusive for anything they can find that might convict someone against any Roman law. We lived a life of fear all the time and were always ordered about outside our homes and conducting business or walking down the street. Since I was a very young woman, I was sheltered from much of the abuse that the men in our community had to suffer. Abuse was constant. That was our men that suffered the most.

I met Joseph from friends of ours and we became enchanted with each other. For to me he looked like a very kind caring person who would make a very good father and family man. Over a long period of time, we grew to know each other very deeply and became very close. Our love grew healthy and pure, and we wanted to be married in the traditional Hebrew fashion and build a life together.

Then one evening as I was getting ready for bed an angel appeared to me. It was extremely frightening to me to have this glowing white angel magically appear in my room when I was getting ready for bed. The Angels first words were:

Dear Mary, you have found great favor in the eyes of God. It is the will of God that you bear a child that will redeem all mankind from their sins. You shall name Him Jesus. Are you willing my dear child to do this for your Father?

Was so stunned I could not talk. I was trembling even though the angel projected such great love toward me and his voice was so calm to me. This experience for me came instantly and suddenly out of nowhere and I never suspected anything like this could ever happen to anyone much less me. I sat there speechless for a time and God's angel patiently waited and his demeanor was so soothing and loving that it allowed me to settle down a little bit and gather my thoughts.

My mind was such that I got confused about everything due to the appearance of God's angel and I really did not think very well. After a time, my hands reduced their vibration a little and I started to get a little bit calmer but really not that much. The Angels light that came from Him was so bright that I thought other people would come rushing into my room wondering what that great light was and where it was coming from. I thought someone would come bursting into my room at any second. But no one came and that frightened me because I was all alone.

I could hear beautiful music in the background. I did not know where it came from but it seemed to gently flood my room and with God's angel being there with this calm and soothing music, I thought that just perhaps this could be indeed an angel of God. And just perhaps what the angel said to me and asked me could actually be for real.

After a while longer my mind started to settle down more and I began to think more clearly about the situation I now found myself in. With the angel and even with the light so bright coming from Him it did not bother my eyes. He certainly lit up the entire room full of a white light that was actually comforting and after a while I began to enjoy that. The angel was smiling at me I could see his face and it was so pure and smooth that I felt like yes this is an angel of God.

Then I began to realize that God is indeed asking me to be with his child that will save humanity from its sinful existence. My faith in Yahweh has always been strong and I loved reading the books that we have that were written by Moses and others. My family shared those books when we wanted to read. So, after more time had passed, I then believed that what the angel had asked me was indeed true. Will I accept Yahweh's offer to be with child that would save humanity from its sinful existence? The words of "yes I will" were on my tongue and they stayed there for moments longer before I actually spoke them. For I knew my life would change forever and that did scare me.

I wanted to be married with Joseph. Now everything was in the air. Then after a little more time of me thinking about this and the angel looking at me with a very nice, pleasant smile on his face, I could feel the love emanating from this angel that it was proper and just for me to say yes to our God in Heaven. So, I told the angel, "yes I will". The angel then said, "you are a beautiful child of your Heavenly Father and He will be exceedingly pleased for your decision."

Do not worry about Joseph for He will be spoken to by your Father very soon and He will come to understand that this is come upon you. You are very blessed my dear Mary and although you will suffer in the times ahead you have found great favor with Almighty God and He will protect you through your entire life. Stay calm dear child and go to sleep now and wake up tomorrow morning refreshed and secure in knowing what your future holds for you. "I will now go to your Father and complete my mission for He already knows your answer and is indeed very well pleased. With the glory of God and his blessings be with you always."

And with that the angel ascended through the roof and upward to where I do not know. This is the story dear Richard of what happened when I was told becoming with child named Jesus.

ANGEL DEPARTS OUR BLESSED MOTHER MARY

Note: The English words and sentences are not completely correct. But they are what Mother Mary said to me, and I did the best I could to get what she said into the computer file as she said them to me.

After God's angel departed from Mary:

Question: dear blessed Mother Mary, could you please comment on what happened after the angel departed from your room, what happened next, when did you tell Joseph, and what was his response? I apologize if this is too personal, and I will not ask it again. It would help the revelation of this book, but again I respect if you say no.

Oh, my dear child thank you for being so respectful loving and understanding. I will not withhold things from you for your heart is pure and your intentions are very good and blessed by your Father in Heaven. So. I will tell you something that characterize what happened immediately after.

I sat on the edge of the bed for a long time trying to understand what just happened. It was so enormous in my mind that it took a long time. My mind was swirling every which way trying to take in what just happened and I was having a hard time understanding all of it. The question came to my mind, "why me". Why of all the so faithful other women in our tribe why was it me that Almighty God would choose for such an enormous assignment.

I did not understand at all my dear Richard. I could not fathom or start out in my mind how all of this fit together then I became very afraid of the future. Even though the angel told me do not fear, I could not help myself, but they certainly did. I was so frightened that I almost felt like throwing up. In that sense it was a terrible experience.

But to you Richard I have to emphasize that I was still filled with the glory, the most beautiful and penetrating love that enveloped me after the angel went away. I have experienced the love of my family and my friend's, but this goes legions beyond anything I experienced until the angel came. The feelings that I experienced were so pleasurable, so great, so accepting and warm and soft and understanding that I wish I could have lived like that for the rest of my life. After the angel left these most wonderful feelings within me started to fade away, I noticed this and I wanted to make them stay somehow but they kept getting weaker and weaker as my mind started to clarify things a little bit for me.

Somewhere during the night, I became so exhausted and so very tired that I lay down on my bed and just thought about what had happened and worried about what would come. I was so afraid of what would come in spite of the assurance God's angel gave me. Then I do not know when I fell asleep until the morning time. When I woke up, I could hear clattering around other parts of our house meaning my family has started to arise and perhaps some food was being prepared. When I left my bedroom, I did not know what to say, what to do, or anything like that.

It was Elizabeth that noticed there was something much different about me than the day before. I did not know what she meant by this. I told her I felt the same but she insisted that something was very different about me. I did not want to talk about it then for I guess I was still recovering from such an enormous event in my life. I ate something and then I went to pray.

It was a few days later that I approached Joseph and I told him what had happened with the angel. But he looked at me very lovingly but he was ever so concerned about what it would look like to the rest of the community. He thought that we should not be married under those circumstances. This broke my heart for I did love Joseph very much.

Somewhere along the line another angel appeared to Joseph and told him that I was with child by the will of Almighty God and I did nothing wrong or I was still a virgin. After some time past we both realized the importance of what had happened and we were married. I think dear Richard this is what you wanted to know and I thank you for writing this book and telling my story.

As revealed by our Blessed Mother Mary to me personally. I cannot describe to you dear reader the great joy and fulfillment I experienced in having our Blessed Mother Mary reveal her magnificent story.

OUR BLESSED MOTHER MARY - THE BIRTH OF JESUS

Question my dear Mother Mary:
I would love to know the details of your journey when Jesus was about to be born and why you were traveling in such a state and also, my dear Mother, please describe your accommodations and the birth of our Lord and Savior Jesus of Nazareth becoming Christ, the son of God and Savior of mankind.

Oh, my dear son, that is a mouthful. As you suggest I will begin when we were on the journey because of the census that was being taken at the command of the emperor. The journey for me was extremely difficult and painful. I was very afraid of all the jostling and swaying back-and-forth would cause some harm to my dear child and as you know the Bible states correctly that we could not find accommodations because everybody was traveling around to their home city.

The people we encountered were kind and understanding to us. Many of them offered for us in any way they could which was very limited at the time. Joseph especially was very tired and getting weaker as we trudged along. One innkeeper told us that there was a barn across the way that was good and sturdy and housed a number of different animals, but there was space for us and our needs.

After we settled down for the night, I started to feel the birthing starting to take place. For me because of God's wonderful grace it was not painful like other women who have experienced the same thing. God is so very good to us that He did not allow any commotion as we journeyed along the road. And now God is showing his love again for us in particular for I really had no terrible pangs of birth. Our Lord and Savior was born in the same manner as all other healthy children are.

Yes, we were in a barn or what the Bible says a stable. And yes, there was a lot of hay all over the place for the animals residing inside. We did have enough food for us because of what Joseph had packed before we left and the small amounts of food, we gathered along the way from the innkeepers that had pity on us and wanted to help. I know they would have given us a room inside their building if they could. They were so kind and as generous as they could toward us and for that they are blessed.

The time was very short from when I noticed the birthing was starting to take place until our Lord Jesus was born. He did not cry at all as what I thought most babies do, He was very content and in need of my milk and we put sacks and other cloth materials around Him to keep Him warm. Oh, my dear Richard, it is such a wonderful memory for me when I first was able to carry Him in my arms. Tears of joy and happiness were flowing down my cheeks as I gazed into his little eyes and then I knew that yes this is indeed God's child of mercy toward all humans in our world. The amount of joy and love that I felt was second only to the appearance of the angel that came to me a lot of months ago.

My pregnancy was not that difficult. It is as if my little baby already knew me and was so comfortable inside me that He did not thrash around inside the womb like many of the other women who were with child told me about. He was born sometime in the evening or early night. I do not feel that is of much importance but I want to be complete with you, my son. After our child Jesus was born and things settle down a bit, a great sense of tiredness mixed with joy and happiness came upon us and we all fell asleep including my little baby boy. We stayed at that place for a number of days afterward for neither Joseph nor I wanted to take a very newly born child onto the road and expose Him to all that come with going from here to there.

When Jesus was an infant, I knew He was hungry when He would whimper and then whimper again. He never really cried out loud much at all. It was such a wonderful little infant to take care of. He was any woman's dream to have a child like Him.

After perhaps a week we had gathered enough food from innkeepers and passersby that we kept with us and by then we felt that our little baby Jesus was now strong enough to allow us to journey onward to our destination. My dear son, that is really about all there was. With the exception that three men of honor did visit us and told us about a star that they were following that led them to where Jesus was born. They did give us gifts each of them and for that we very much appreciated. It really doesn't matter what they gave us but they were of very good value and it came out of their deep love of our God in Heaven that they travel very far to see our most beautiful child.

I do not know what else is important to tell you about other than that is the story of our journey back home and how we stopped along the way encountered very kind and loving people and when we resumed our journey back home. Thank you for asking these lovely questions my dear son. I am always with you and will always be with you forever. I love you.

Question: My dearest blessed Mother Mary, I hope I am not pushing things too far, for I do not want to wear out my welcome. You have been enormously kind, gentle, and understanding regarding the questions I have asked you. The book of Thomas is not part of Biblical literature, as we both know. However, sometimes non Biblical literature contains some truth, and I wonder if you can comment about that book and if there is anything in it that is true. If you say no, I will completely understand and honor your wishes.

Oh, my dear child, you have hit upon a sore spot for me because the book of Thomas was written by some monks long after of our Lord and its Savior Jesus Christ. They got that information from dribbles and drabs that were floating around and then they amplified it to a great degree. They wanted to portray my son, Jesus, as an ordinary boy growing up with magical powers that He could not control and did things that were terribly wrong against the wishes of our Father in Heaven. That book my dear son, belongs in the garbage for it contains no truth.

There are many other books that have been written about my son after His ascension into Heaven and they are varying degrees much the same as the book of Thomas. I believe the church in its early years the day magnificent and wonderful job of searching out which writings were true and factual about the life and teachings of my son and your Savior while throwing away the writings that were not inspired by our Father in Heaven. I am very happy that the Bible as it stands today across the world is a very close representation of the times, the events, and the teachings of my son Christ.

It is the Bible so many different languages and having so many different ways of expressing the basic truths of our Almighty Father in Heaven and Jesus. Thank you for asking this question dear Richard. I know you will pass this on to many Christian people that will absorb this truth and apply it within their sacred lives.

Are there any other points of formation you want to tell their readers of this book?

There are so many things I could say but your book would turn into an encyclopedia. For now, I am completely satisfied have already written and I know what it is you are planning to write in addition. So, unless other questions come to your mind that you feel would add to my story or related things, please ask me and I will reveal to you personally what my response would be I love you dear Richard for all that you are doing for God's children.

ON JESUS BECOMING HUMAN

Question: My dear Lord and Savior, I never thought in my entire life that I would ever have the opportunity while on earth, at least to ask you this question. But here I am. My question is, what was it like for you to become human in all respects? Yes, Christians know you were fully human and divine while with us on earth 2000 years ago. But for you as part of the Trinity, what was it like for your existence to be so limited as a human on earth?

September 9, 2022, 04.56 PM
Jesus Christ

My dear son this is the first time that I have ever addressed this kind of question with one of God's sacred children as you are. My dear son you are special among your Father's children and you do not know the wonders that are waiting for you.

That being said I did go through all of the sensations, the physical sensations and much of the emotional experiences as well for being born as a human being on the earth. Most of my powers, my unlimited powers as a member of the Trinity were not purposely available to me. But the ones that remained with me were far beyond what any human being can imagine.

It was early on after your Father in Heaven created all of his children in a blink of an eye and after you and the rest of his children were spiritual beings residing in the Heavenly Kingdom with your Father as was described elsewhere in your book, we knew that it was necessary for me the only begotten son within the Trinity would need to come to earth to repair the damage that one of our angels would do in the future against all sacred children. This was many eons before the earth was formed and the general spiritual realm that exists in harmony with the physical realm.

This is also discussed elsewhere in your book. You purposely do not remember all the great experiences the Trinity had with your Father's sacred spiritual children. Before you came to earth this was erased from your minds but it will return when you return to the Heavenly Kingdom.

As a child growing up in Nazareth with St. Joseph and the Blessed Mother Mary, I did have to go through all the normal human sensations and feelings as any normal child. And this continued as I got older. However deep within me was how you would say the other me, the completely divine me as well. It was very difficult for me to have given up for example the power that I had where all I would need to do to create whatever it is they wished was to think it into existence. I did not have that as a child or adult for that would be disastrous to my mission of salvation for all of Almighty God's sacred children.

All the limitations of the human body were excruciating for me as the infinitely powerful spiritual being without limitations. Yet this experience was also ever so fulfilling and loving in a different way within my existence. The love within the Trinity is infinitely total between us and now I was experiencing a different kind of love between the physicality of God's children on earth. It is a far different experience both in character and intensity for me.

I was also experiencing for the first time human emotions that I did have difficulty with growing up as a child and into adulthood. Yet at the same time by experiential knowledge of firsthand contact with other totally human children increased greatly and my love for each child of God became more refined and accepting and understanding what each different child can see within this physical reality we created.

The pressures of providing for your own existence and survival on earth is unheard of in the spiritual Kingdom. Being exposed to that gives far greater meaning to the love and devotion that most of God's children have for each other. The idea of sacrificing for the other through love is a virtue beyond compare and it gives me and your Father and the Holy Spirit a magnificent sense of fulfillment and love for each one of God's sacred children.

There is no substitute for firsthand experience through the eyes of God's children for it is within that where love, forgiveness, sacrifice, and faith are realized to the fullest extent in the minds of us within the Trinity. It is a magnificent feeling that I felt was very much worth all the pain I knew I would suffer to create a pathway back to Almighty God in the Trinity for each one of his sacred children if they so choose to use it.

My dear son there is ever so much more that I could tell you about how an infinite being experiences becoming ever so physically limited on earth as you are today. But dear son, remember that because all that you have done and what you have promised and delivered on before you were born there are wonderments for you to enjoy beyond anything you can imagine waiting for you when your mission is finished on this earth.

Thank you, dear Lord. That is such an overwhelming and wonderful answer to my question. I love you so very much, and I know you will continue being by my side for the rest of my days.

27

Jesus Travels with His Godly Message

Jesus' missing years, where He went, and what He did. There is so much speculation about the missing years before the crucifixion of our Lord and Savior. Here, we all have a 100% summary of what He did along with his traveling companions, where they went, what they did and what they said, etc. They had many suffering and challenges along the way, but they survived for all the years they were away.

September 27, 2022
Jesus Christ

My dearest child, yes you are legally right in your thoughts about me and my psychological makeup where I am the only person in existence where I as 100% powerful God and 100% human being has the psychological makeup of the interior interface of God. Aristotle, Freud, and many of the magnificent psychoanalysts to analyze me for there is a rich field of view that could be analyzed but no matter how hard they could analyze it would always be incomplete. This is because both the human mind and certainly the Godly mind has a quality of depth that is ceaseless for it is not only three-dimensional, but it is forth fifth sixth and past the X and onward.

For it has no end. And yes, it is true for the human mind as well because you were made that way. You my dear child are far more complex than you yourselves can ever know. Yet there are obvious places where on the surface inside our minds there are places where we need lovingly so that there are not conflicts but love and joy. These places are ones that produce just that, love and joy and a wonderment for your Father and Me and the Holy Spirit which proceeds from Us. And through time these places will grow deeper and deeper.

As they mature for nothing in this universe is static everything grows and matures. We designed it that way. This is why inherent deserts there are times when botanists will find some moss growing on rocks that should not be there but are. They are special indeed.

The words of your Heavenly Father were very much like the moss. They were planted in the desert. Yet they grew in the hearts of many different people in very hot places. None of the places that I spoke were fertile grounds people. All were hostile environments where the people all had strong beliefs in pagan gods created by man that were earthly in nature. All were hostile gods that if you disobeyed, then you would be killed and so on. If you disobeyed the gods there was either torture, losing a limb, or being killed as a sacrifice. There were also series of punishments of banishment where you would be thrown out of the tribe into the desert where within days you would starve from lack of water and have thirst.

HIS FAITHFUL COMPANIONS

All of these different tribes were not so different really. They were all very hierarchical. All had a chief and sub chiefs in charge of different duties then after that some type of lieutenant that certain work would be done by other workers. The rise to becoming a chief was by means of a family. The idea of voting for chief was unheard of.

My message to all of these chiefs who were very egocentric was simple. I talked about one great and powerful chief that lived among the stars. This great chief created the stars and the earth. This great chief created the earth and He created the mountains and the waters.

And if they asked, I told them that He created all of us humans. He created us a very long time ago. And He sent me to tell everyone that He loves all of us very much. I told Him also that He forbids everyone to hurt anyone else. That it is a great sin to hurt anyone to kill anyone and harm anyone else. This great chief of the stars demands that you help everyone else even your enemies. And so, I told them of the 10 Commandments at this point I levitated about 10 feet above the ground when I told him of the commandments, they needed to see something that they would remember.

HIS MISSING YEARS, WHERE HE WENT AND WHAT HE DID

As I traveled to other tribes, some were more open, intelligent and a little more sophisticated and I would speak a little differently to them. I would speak more as I would to the Hebrews however no matter where I went, I always felt the need to levitate so they would always remember me as the person that would levitate and tell them about the great God that lived among the stars and proved to them how powerful He was and how good He was. I asked the scribe within each tribe to write down what I said. Each tribe always had a scribe so I did leave behind written material as best he could. This also was very important.

The Holy Spirit was with each tribe after I left and was there with the scribe and the people after I left and assisted especially the scribe assisting Him with what he was writing to ensure what he wrote was good and accurate. Nothing could be better than getting assistance from the Holy Spirit. There are no errors left when written with help of the Holy Spirit.

There were also times along my journeys when there were people that fell in love with my message from God and they asked if they could spread to other parts of the territories that I was not planning to go to and I said to them yes and after a time I would go one way or another with their entourage and so the Holy Spirit went with them and went with me what a wonderful happening. Remember dear child the Holy Spirit can be anywhere He wishes so being multidimensional is never a problem. The Holy Spirit went with the both of us and this is a wonderful blessing. This happened more than once. Most people think that it was only me but it's me plus one. The newly formed group went to the North where I continued more to the east for the remainder of our trip.

For each of us there usually was a total of four or five in our group. We usually had protective gear if it rained and food if we got hungry. And we had stuff necessary to make a small fire to keep us warm. Yes, I am God and could provide that all by myself but it's appropriate not to do that kind of thing.

People do not know the story of the man who went north and broke away from our group of people. For that matter people do not even know of our trip for that matter. All they know is that I disappeared for about 20 years from the Bible and reappeared when I reentered Jerusalem. I would like to say a few things about the man that broke away from our group of people while we were on this trip informing so many people about our Father in Heaven that created all that is seen and unseen and everyone on the earth that loves us so very much.

People on this trip need to know who their Father is so they can stop worshiping pagans and idol gods that are false images that lead them nowhere. They do this out of complete ignorance. They need to worship the one and only true God. There is a true Father in Heaven. These people are ignorant, and we must set them free from their ignorance.

Then my gospel travels began my dear son. I was only 13 years old. It was after I preached on the steps of the temple. You already know what I said to my Hebrew friends. My words are recorded in the Old Testament. After that the Bible does not record any of my activities it goes silent. So much speculation about where I went. I left out of Jerusalem and a very long trip preaching about our Father in Heaven, about the Ten Commandments and about what is found in Biblical ethics and morality. You will find the last two areas spread throughout several books in the Bible. Not like the 10 Commandments as given by Moses.

I want to tell his story now. His name is Banji. Banji was a very interesting man. He thought it would be interesting for his group to travel north and bring the word, the new Word of God and all the things he heard about God to the people in the north. He figured out that there was an ocean to his left and when his adventures were done, he could take left turn and return over the water back to Jerusalem in some manner over a period of time and there would be less danger that way. He was very smart and would be back home again.

And it thrilled him to be preaching the word that he believed in more and more every time he heard what the word of God was because in his mind the pieces were coming together better and better. He was figuring things out and believed the entire gospel. I could see it in his eyes and I could see his mind working and it was a wonderful sight for me. He was a very good man inside his soul. I saw him one more time back in Jerusalem and his mission in the north was a very good success. It was a few days before I was crucified. He had returned a number of months before I did. I was waiting for him in Heaven.

You could say that Banji was one of the very first missionaries for our Heavenly Father. In fact, I say he was the first. he preached a very basic message that I personally gave him and people responded to him because of his personality and his heart of love and pure enjoyment of what he was doing for the people he was talking to. He was a great man and a great friend that I thoroughly enjoyed welcoming him through the great gates of the Heavenly realm.

At this point I believe this is the end of my story regarding where I went on my journey after I left the Biblical account of my life and now the Bible begins.

28

Jesus Arrives in Jerusalem and The Crucifixion

This section addresses the time from immediately before Jesus enters Jerusalem until He rises from the tomb and returns to his disciples. This part of our sacred Bible is the focal point for all Christianity. If these events did not happen, especially when Jesus rose from the dead, all belief in Christianity would crumble beneath our feet. There are many things and many books that have been written about these events. What you are about to read are the insider comments and messages that God Almighty wants to emphasize for your spiritual well-being and to give you the strength and encourage your faith that these events actually did happen.

September 9, 2022, 10:43 AM
Jesus Christ

I knew since I was an adolescent what the trajectory of my life on earth would be. I knew that it would culminate with my assassination by the religious leaders of the time due to their rejection of God's true words to his people. I like you dear son was a messenger from our Holy Father in Heaven. As is the case with so many children, they were bound tightly by their preconceived notions of what God is and what they think God is not.

For many generations of the Hebrew people, they have been waiting for the Messiah to come and free them from the tyranny of Roman rule. They thought that the Messiah would come as a great spiritual and military leader that would galvanize the people to rise up and destroy the Roman legions that surrounded them. This would involve huge amounts of wholesale killing.

This is certainly not what their Heavenly Father is and certainly not what I am. I brought them peace and the education that their real home is not of this earth but rather is of the Heavenly Kingdom. I told them many times that whosoever believe in me shall not perish but have everlasting life. Many people thought that meant they would live forever on earth but that is certainly not true. Everlasting life means they will live in a place with their Father in the Heavenly Kingdom, and they would live forever in peace, harmony with bountiful joy and love surrounding them always.

I am not a bringer of war. I am a bringer of good news to the Hebrew people and entire world. This is something that is antithetical to their preconceived notions of what their Messiah be like. I was the opposite. I am the Son of Man and I am the Son of God. For I am fully human and I am fully God. It is I that forms the bridge, the gateway, the sacred connection between our Heavenly Father, the Holy Kingdom in Heaven and God's sacred children on earth. This is something that the religious leaders refused to accept. They rejected me also for the reason of envy and sensing a diminution of their religious and political power within the social structure of the Hebrew people as it related to the Roman occupiers.

So with this in mind, I knew that once I entered Jerusalem for the last time I would be crucified by the Sanhedrin in an illegal way and as approved by the Roman authorities who decided to take a hands-off position for political reasons.

When I arrived in Jerusalem, I chose a donkey to ride into the gate. Military people ride horses. I chose a donkey because I am a bringer of peace and love for all humanity. It was a wonderful feeling for me to be accepted so enthusiastically by so many of God's sacred children. For they have a simple yet loving mindset in their hearts and truly are always looking toward their Father in Heaven.

Those of the Sanhedrin however have replaced the simplicity and honesty of their hearts and minds with the pursuit of earthly pleasures, earthly political power and control as much as possible over the lives of the Hebrew people. It is this urge and mindset of the pursuit political power over God's children that is the same as what is promoted by Satan himself.

Most everything that I said and did upon my arrival in Jerusalem was in fulfillment of the prophecies and scriptures that have been written for the benefit of the Hebrew people. Inwardly I knew that my mission on earth was very close to being finished. It was frustrating for me to be in the midst of so many people that did not come close to understanding my sacred message to them from their Father in Heaven. Most were still unbelieving in spite of what loving messages I told them from their Father, they believed that in a minute how I would turn into a military conqueror for their benefit against the Romans. It seemed as if almost everybody completely misunderstood who I was and what I was there to accomplish.

My dear son, my frustration with the apostles was very great. Although I know the future and how things would turn out the human side of me nonetheless was irritated and yes frustrating. I had hoped that they would've understood deeply inside them far more than what they displayed on the surface. You my dear son Richard have understood in far more detail and truthfulness what my message was then and still is today. My mission could be described as what is read in the Bible. I am the way the truth and the life. No one goes to the Father except by me.

After Adam and Eve, all of God's sacred children were broken away from Him because of the inherited stain of serious sin by their two ancestors Adam and Eve. Not only was my mission here to bring to our Father's children a far greater understanding of what Heaven is like, what it takes to go to the Father and what behavioral rules must be followed in order to regain your Father's Heavenly blessing. My mission was and remains to bring Heavenly truth to all that will listen and make the effort to understand.

But in addition to this and just as important there did remain a broken spiritual linkage between our Father's children and our Almighty Father himself. This linkage is within the spiritual realm. Remember that almost all of creation is within the spiritual realm not the physical. The physical is necessary so that God's children may exist on planet Earth which provides them an opportunity to prove to themselves and their Father in Heaven that they are worthy of regaining their spiritual blessings that were lost by Adam and Eve. And to prove that they can withstand the evils and wretchedness of the adversary formally known as Lucifer the morning Star now known as Satan the evil one.

So, first I came to give the good news of what we call the gospel. Secondly out of sight of most everybody comes from the fact that I was fully God and fully human at the same time. Within me dear son, existed and still exists and always will exist the vastly important linkage, the spiritual linkage, the emotional linkage between Almighty God's sacred children and the Heavenly Kingdom. By believing in my message and believing in who I am that linkage gets extended to all those, believe in me and my message and those who act out in their life the outward actions that they take within their lives to prove to all the universe, to prove to themselves and to prove to our Almighty Father in Heaven that they indeed are worthy of rejoining their Father in the Heavenly Kingdom.

There are a few unfortunately who will succeed in this because <u>Satan appeals to their lower instincts of selfishness, greed, and all the other human tendencies and frailties that have been handed down throughout the generations that started with Adam and Eve and manifested itself horrifically in the actions of Cain and his murder of Abel.</u>

One of the reasons that there are so many of God's children that will not make it back to Him in the Heavenly Kingdom is that Satan works full-time in terribly deceitful ways, in any way possible to slowly chip away at the God-given nature of his children that they have at birth. It is so easy for negligent and what you call now secular parents to commit so many sins of neglect or outright cruelty to their children when they're young. This damages their children for the rest of their children's lives in this damage then generates more negative impulses and emotions of the subsequent parents onto the next generation of innocent children.

I know dear son Richard that you have experienced this in very harsh detail while you were growing up. It took you six years of intense work on your part to break away from the damage your parents have caused you. My dear son you have is your counselor once told you, you have broken the chain within your family. Your children are far better off than you ever were.

It is my fervent desire that all of your Fathers' children follow your example while you are on the earth. But you dear son and I know far better than this. Almighty God could command that everyone act in a holy and sacred manner. But this will never happen because it would violate one of the rock solid characteristics of all of your Father in Heaven gifts to all his children. That is the gift of complete free will. It is in this way that those who love the Trinity will have done so from their own free will, from their own free choice.

This is the desire of all three of us in the Trinity. This is completely opposite to the domination, control, the sinister and ugly tactics of Satan and his demons. If you want to discern on earth who is a follower of the Trinity in love, peace and fulfillment just look at their behavior and you  *will find out very quickly whose destiny is the Heavenly Kingdom or the disintegrating and dissolving hell into nothingness.*

Getting back to my beautiful apostles, there was a few fleeting moments on my human side that became very concerned about my message being able to be continued throughout the subsequent generations into the future. But quickly my sacred side knew that would never happen in my message would be solidified for all those generations yet to come. And that my up-and-coming crucifixion would be eternally successful.

But that being said, even my apostles after being with me for a little over three years did not fully comprehend what I had taught them and what I have done in the healing of people and my message to them. I told my disciples more than three times as is shown in the Bible that I would be crucified very shortly in fulfillment of the Scriptures. Most of them shook their head and did not want to believe that what happened in spite of me telling them so.

Upon my arrival through the gates of Jerusalem there were so many people ever so happy to see me and threw flowers and good wishes toward me after laying palm leaves in front of my path. This was a wonderful experience for me in spite of what was coming. The next day I went to the temple to pray and I found it had been turned into a marketplace. The moneychangers were particularly offensive against our Father in Heaven. There were a few Roman guards and lookouts from the Pharisees, the Sanhedrin that were observing what I did to the people, moneychangers, and other sellers of goods in the temple. They did nothing to stop me because they did not want to start a riot nor did I.

Later that evening it was arranged that my apostles and I and a close group of loyal friends would have food together after the sunset in the garden of Gethsemane. It was there that I knew one of the 12 would betray me and have me handed over to the Sanhedrin. At our last supper one of the apostles, Judas, would sneak away and inform the agents of the Sanhedrin where I was that evening. He led them back to me and betrayed me with a kiss. All of this is accurately accounted for in your New Testament of the Bible.

29

The Crucifixion

Later in the deep hours of the night I was questioned by the members of the Sanhedrin. It was plain and obvious to discern that they are doing everything in their power to entrap me into saying something that would give them any excuse to put me to death. All their minds were roiling with inventing as many angles as they could in their feeble minds to create anything that they could think of to condemn me. They even asked me whether I paid a poll tax. If I said yes then the people would say I am not the Messiah. If I said no then I would be admitting I committed treason against the Roman authorities.

I could feel the glee in their minds when Josephus asked Me that. Instead, I told them that since the likeness of Caesar was on the coins to give unto Caesar what Caesar's. And to give unto God what is God's. With that they became filled with rage against me and then turned me over to Herod for him to execute me.

But Herod and his questioning of me could find no legal fault. All throughout this episode, this circus, the agents of the Sanhedrin were stirring up the people to be against me with false accusations. They started to chant the words, "crucify Him, crucify Him". Herod on the other hand did not want my blood on his hands and yes, it is true that he washed his hands in a bowl of water to show his disgust with the Pharisees and the Sanhedrin who were adamant for my death.

Later, Pilate did what is documented in the New Testament Gospels of my apostles. The maddening crowd chose Barabbas the criminal to be set free due to the holiday that was eminent. So, in order to keep some semblance of peace this is what he did. I was turned over to the Roman guards, was tortured and kept in a jail cell until the next morning when I was whipped and a crown of thorns were not only placed on my head but rather pounded into my head. At this point my body was bleeding from everywhere and the pain is something not describable in human words. The worst part for me was all the taunts, all the spitting at me and so on.

I was made to drag my cross up to the hill of execution. There were two others already hung on their crosses. The Gospels describe what happened next. As I told you earlier dear son, I was on the cross for a total of 3.8 hours. During that time dear son, the physical pain was not increasing anymore. Rather it seemed that it was subsiding as time went on. Such is one of the blessings from the way we in the Trinity designed the human body for its purpose to be a vehicle that allows God's sacred children to choose if they wish to spend eternity with us in the Heavenly Kingdom or not. I know this is covered elsewhere in this beautiful book you are writing.

I was coming into and out of consciousness for the last hour or so on the cross. My vision was getting blurred, and I could not see the people around me like I could before. Your blessed Mother Mary and Mary Magdalene and others close to me were there. None of my apostles were visible to me for they became frightened out of their minds about what was happening.

The most painful part of all of this for me was when your Father in Heaven turned his back on me and I could no longer feel Him being an integral part of my existence. To understand this agony of not sensing or feeling our Almighty Father, I offer you these following thoughts. Within the Trinity we are both one and three intimately together in every aspect of existence. Nothing happens to the one that does not happen to the three. Yet at the same time we as three derive most delicious and fulfilling joy, love, and happiness when we explore the infinite depths of each other in so many different ways. I talk about this in other parts of your book my dear son. Thankfully the hell of experiencing the absence of your Father in Heaven was not too long. Immediately after that I ascended out of my body. This was not visible to the people that surrounded my crucifixion. But before I left, I did say: "IT IS FINISHED". And so, it was.

And so, I was successful in reconnecting the spiritual breakage between your Almighty Father in Heaven and all His children, His sacred children on earth. Now all that was left is for each individual sacred child to decide if they wish to return back to the Heavenly Kingdom and live all eternity with all three of us especially your Father in the Heavenly Kingdom where there are no limitations.

The end of the greatest and most important events in human history and the beginning of the brightest and most loving endless stories for God's sacred children are yet to come

And so, this ends our discussion of the most important events in human history. It is the birth, the life, the death and the ascension of our Lord and Savior Jesus Christ. Always remember that during his life, Jesus of Nazareth became Jesus the Christ. And in doing so He reestablished the pathway for you and me to return to our Father in the Kingdom of Heaven. Remember too that all of us lived with our Father in the Heavenly Kingdom for eons of time before we came to this earth to make the decision where will we spend the rest of eternity. This decision would never have been necessary were it not for the free will choices of Lucifer the morning Star rebelling against the sacred Trinity and the horrible choices of Adam and Eve.

Our loving Father created the stars above and the earth under our feet and our one-of-a-kind personal bodies that all match perfectly together so that we may choose to live with our Father and the Trinity for all endless time to come. In Jesus name, Amen.

30

Further Commentary

As our loving Father in Heaven has stated that I am his anointed messenger, I would be remiss in ending this theological work of truth at this point without further commentary. It is highly appropriate that a commentary be attached for further truthful realizations and learning about the material you have just read. And I will do so starting now.

THE CRUCIFIXION OF JESUS CHRIST

Please forgive me when I tell you that I did not want to write this section of this book. The thought of what the Romans did to our Lord and Savior distresses me greatly. As for me, given the chance, I would have personally hung each member of the Sanhedrin from the ceiling by their personal parts not fit for print. Yes, I know that's an improper sentence in this beautiful theology book. But we are in a section of the book depicting ugly reality, so sometimes I let loose my animal instincts, and this is what comes out.

Years ago, I purposely avoided watching the horrifically violent depiction of the crucifixion in Mel Gibson's movie "The Passion Of The Christ." Others that saw the movie told me of the detailed and violent depictions of Christ's sufferings.

I'm glad I did not see the movie. My Christian spiritual advisor was obligated to see the movie because of all her other clients that saw it. She described in great horrific and gory detail the pathetic awful lengths Mel Gibson went to amplify the agony, the blood in ripping the flesh out of His body of our Lord and Savior Jesus Christ. Knowing that Americans love blood and gore in their movies, Gibson provided their lust and taste for as much red blood as he could throw at them.

1950'S STYLE UNDERSTANDING REGARDING THE BLOOD OF JESUS

All this brought back memories of my sophomore year at Santa Clara University in theology class when the Jesuit professor kept pounding on the fact that we are all forgiven because of **THE BLOOD, THE BLOOD, THE BLOOD, THE BLOOD**! I will never forget that Catholic priest's name, Father Androdi. If there was any priest that was an effective Catholic faith repellent of the faith, this guy was certainly it. I'm glad for undergraduate school at Santa Clara University, I only had to endure five quarterly classes in theology so I would not have to put up with Jesuits like this man.

Now, if you need an example of a miracle, you certainly can use me. I was forced to go to parochial school for five years at St. Tarcissus in Chicago, Illinois, where I was subjected to really bad, mean, and cruel nuns imported directly from Germany right after losing World War II to our parents. This was in 1953 when Germany got its butt kicked in 1945, only eight years earlier, so their hatred was very fresh in their minds, and they were determined to seek revenge on the children of the soldiers that beat the snot out of their military.

But, among the tasks that have been asked of me to do by Almighty God, I have been told to write this part. So, I will. Besides, I know this book will not be complete unless I do write this. As in all the rest of this book, I will have great help and historically correct detailed information consistent with the Biblical accounts. They certainly will be because the source of the information you are about to read is from our loving Almighty Father. What you are going to read goes into greater detail further than the accounts in the New Testament.

WHY THE CRUCIFIXION HAD TO HAPPEN

The crucifixion of God's only begotten son, Jesus Christ, was a pivotal event in human history. That event created the final piece of the pathway back to Almighty God for his sacred children. God created both the spiritual realm and the physical realm in such a way as to perfectly match the designed bodies of his children. Simply put, God's sacred children occupied bodies containing full spiritual and physical functionality. This is described in another part of this book. Jesus was and remains the link between us human beings and the Heavenly Kingdom. Always remember what Jesus Christ told us," no one can go to the Father except through me." "I am the way, the truth, and the life." These are very powerful words.

Always remember that Jesus Christ is fully human and, at the same time, fully divine. Jesus was born into this world in the same manner all the rest of God's children were born. But He was born without original sin that happened when Adam and Eve ate the fruit from the tree of the knowledge of good and evil. Additionally, Jesus was fully divine or, more accurately, fully God. Remember, Jesus was fully God and created the universe.

Now within the only begotten son of God, Jesus provided the linkage or the connection between Almighty God and his human sacred children. Because Jesus was both, Jesus was both a human and God together. Through Him, the linkage between our almighty Father in Heaven and his sacred children was re-established from the brokenness created by Adam and Eve so long ago.

There was a penalty, a price to be paid for the sin committed by Adam and Eve. As it was in Hebrew society, small animals were sacrificed to pay for transgressions. Keeping with this long-standing tradition, our Lord and Savior Jesus Christ became known as the sacrificial Lamb. This is because He allowed himself to be sacrificed on a cross. So Almighty God and his sacred children could be reconciled with the Trinity and regain the possibility of eternal life in paradise with their Father in the Heavenly Kingdom. All the sacred children needed to do was follow the 10 Commandments given by Moses generations earlier and accept our Lord and Savior Jesus Christ for what He is and what He did. Now, his sacred children could choose to return to God our Father by loving Him, having faith in Jesus Christ, and following his commandments while living on earth.

Our Heavenly Father created the spiritual realm in the physical realm that is magnificently fine-tuned to their bodies' spiritual and physical needs. Our Lord and Savior Jesus Christ did two things in general. He founded the Christian church along with his apostles, that would spread the good news across the world. He also died on the cross, which created the unbreakable spiritual link between God's sacred children and the

Heavenly Kingdom. Always remember, my dear Christian, that all of the above I explained had one purpose and one only purpose.

It was to redeem God's sacred children so they may return to Him in the Heavenly Kingdom and live with their Father, his only begotten son, and the Holy Spirit. They will live in all eternity with them in a paradise that they cannot imagine. But the pathway back to the Heavenly Kingdom could not happen in any way if Jesus Christ had not died on the cross and been resurrected three days later.

31

The Ascension of Jesus Christ

My dearest Lord Jesus, I can't believe I left this section to the last part of writing this book. It is the most important of all within our magnificent Christianity. But then again, it can be said that it is the crescendo of everything that is important in all of creation. So please, my dearest Lord and Savior, tell all of your children what it is you feel within this important message you wish to tell about your death and resurrection and return to our Father in the Heavenly realm. Thank you in advance for everything you are about to tell us.

The traditional dates of the crucifixion of our Lord and Savior Jesus Christ on Good Friday and his resurrection on Easter Sunday are incorrect. This can easily be seen because tradition also holds that Jesus Christ was in the tomb for three days and three nights, but the time from Friday to Sunday is only two days. Even a cursory inspection shows this to be horrifically in error.

My dear Lord and Savior: you were crucified three days ago, and then you went to our Heavenly Father, and now you have returned to the physical earth to rejoin your apostles. What a great wretched transition that must've been for you.

PERSONAL COMMENTARY FROM JESUS
I became visible in the room where my apostles were hiding out on the second floor. It was the gathering place where they were so terrified from the Romans that they thought were looking for them. It was a terrible time for them even for the women that were with them. I cannot blame them for I had just been crucified five days earlier and then my body had disappeared, and they were planning some type of an escape themselves and they just did not know what to do or where to go. There are in a deep state of panic and from a human level I could not blame them at all. Everything they believed in was crushed.

All the doors were locked, and they had previously asked that trusted people guard the entryways to the stairs and told them a meeting was going on of some political nature upstairs. And there was some food around the table when I appeared, and the room brightened up because my body was given half a beautiful light with a blue tinge to it. Everyone got very afraid and fell silent. They were completely astonished and had no idea if it was me or not. After a few seconds I said, "peace be with you for it is I."

I stretched out my hands and they could see the holes that were in them. Yes, my dear friends, I have risen, and I am alive just as I said I would. Nobody moved a muscle. It is like they are completely frozen in place. I don't think anyone of them took a breath. I told the twelve don't forget to breathe. Don't pass out on me. Take a deep breath please. It is I your master. It is I Jesus. I told you I would rise from the dead and so I have. I am here with you again. I am with you now. Still, no one talked. So, I sat down on a chair next to them in front and I kept my arms outstretched and looked at them and smiled. They still remained completely astonished and afraid to say anything.

Then I told them what happened. On the third day I rose from the dead in fulfillment of the Scriptures. Then I came back also in fulfillment of the Scripture to be with you, my apostles. I am here in bodily form and after a while they started to speak and remember who I am.

Then they started to have some courage to touch me and to talk. John was the first to talk and offered his hand and I said put your finger through my hand and He saw that his finger went through from one side to the other and so did Bartholomew. After a few minutes all of them had tested my wounds in one way or another but it was Thomas that said He won't believe until he puts his hand into my side and so he did, he said dear Jesus you are my Savior. Then he believed.

The supper with Jesus: It was then that I told the group that I was hungry and could they get me some food. They had some vegetables some bread and fish and I thought that would taste really good because I told them I had not eaten for six days. A few of them laughed and thought that was really funny. I laughed too because yes that was actually quite funny. They brought some wine as well it was a very dark wine and then I told them a joke, I said I wonder if I would leak. Everyone laughed. And the answer is I did not leak anything.

Frankly my dear son, I do not know to this day why I did not leak anything. Who would've thought. The food tasted so good. There was the best food that I've ever had. It is funny how plain food can taste so good. After eating with everybody I told them about how wonderful Heaven really is how they will enjoy Heaven and how it has wonders beyond their imagination. And how there are many people waiting for all of them that they have loved so much on earth that had passed away. But all of them have much work to do before they can see their loved ones in Heaven. As all of us to ask for me I told Him that I will be with them only for a short time and then I will ascend back into Heaven to rejoin my Father.

The apostles did not like that idea, but I told him why, and they understood. After the meal together we needed to make plans for the future. The twelve of us knew each of us had to go our own separate ways where we had to split up into small groups and go different directions to spread what is now called the gospel. We had to agree upon what are the key elements in the message that we needed to tell the world.

We needed to put together the stories of the miracles that I had performed and the healings that I had done for the sick people. We needed to make sure that all of this was represented in a very powerful way. Additionally, needed to make sure that all of the apostles were given the power to do what I had done so that they were my true representative in every way including all the healing and all the miracles as well. This is ever so important. This was going to take some time everything had to be perfect as their Father in Heaven is perfect. There was much joy and fulfillment in preparing for this. There would be four to five people in each group.

Also, each of the disciples had to know what I knew so they could answer all the questions that would come from the people. This would be the hardest thing for each of the apostles. Obviously, they could not know everything I knew so, we attached the apostles' brain to mine regarding this. Meaning if a question came up that they did not know something I would be aware instantly and I would provide the answer to the apostle and so on. Nowadays you would call that the Internet.

Our other long-term challenge was to periodically communicate with each other over long distances. This was a daunting challenge. We very much wanted to know how the others were doing. So, we devised a system where once every couple of months we would send a courier back to Jerusalem with a message stating how we were doing and requests for anything we may need and what kind of help we may need. We also wanted to know how the others were doing and what worked for them and what didn't work as well. Depending on the season it would take anywhere from three to six months on foot or two to four months on muleback.

JESUS ASCENDS TO HEAVEN

After a time, my role on earth was finished. The twelve were ready for their missions and I felt they were all well prepared. It was then we all assembled together there was both happiness and joy along with great sadness for this would be the last time we would assemble like this.

The next time we would be together would be in Heaven in the holiest of all places with a joy and happiness that humans can only imagine. It was then in full view of everyone that I ascended into Heaven with such love in my heart for all my apostles and all those that loved me so very much there were angels all around me as the Heavens opened and we went higher and higher until we could be seen no more.

My mission was complete but remember I would always be with all those that love me for I would never leave them never at all. I love you.

32

Purgatory

I believe that almost every Christian has heard about the place called purgatory. Most people believe it is a temporary place of punishment after death for believers to purge themselves of the last vestiges of sin before they are allowed into the Heavenly realm. This concept of temporary punishment is part of Catholic church doctrine. The problem is that purgatory is NOT a Biblical idea. It was NOT taught by Jesus Christ or the early church. The word purgatory cannot be found anywhere in either the Old Testament or the New Testament. It does NOT exist in Biblical literature.

It is a teaching first expressed by the Roman Catholic Church as early as the Council of Florence (1431 - 1449 A.D.). BUT! This teaching is a man-made doctrine that is warned against in the New Testament labeled the "traditions of men" (Mark 7:8, Colossians 2:8). Mark 7:8 8

As someone with a master's degree in theology and pastoral ministry, it is easy to shoot holes in this so-called teaching or doctrine. The reason is simple. If a Christian repents and is forgiven while alive, there cannot be an ongoing and lingering sin debt. When God forgives, He forgives totally and permanently.

Like many others, the promulgation of this doctrine ultimately obscures the precious truth of the Holy Writ. ALMIGHTY GOD DID NOT CREATE PURGATORY AS PART Of his CREATION PLAN FOR HIS SACRED CHILDREN TO COME BACK TO HIM IN THE HEAVENLY REALM FOR ALL ETERNITY.

So, if God has forgiven you, you cannot have a lingering stain on your soul. Confession and prayer are where forgiveness is granted. Forget purgatory. Just continue to rejoice and be happy that Almighty God loves you more than you can understand.

33

Enter Into the Heavenly Kingdom

A POETIC VIEW

Our new home, God's children succeed

*Forgiven you go to the Heavenly Kingdom, through the Heavenly gate.
God yearns for all to succeed, to join him in the paradise complete,
live with Father for all eternity. Magnificent realm, behold elation,
what a story, live in timeless time, endless joy, and exhilaration
God in His Kingdom. Love, intimacy knowledge, freedom, fun in the city
boundless love we can certainly be.
Be there with the Trinity, Father, Son, and Holy Spirit.
Exciting things await all of us, for you and me.
For children of God that passed earth's tests,
Our eternal destiny is joyous fulfillment you see!
We all will live in Godly truth in the Kingdom creation.
All loving each other sacred children as one loving nation.
Rather now all his peace and loving with work fulfilling,
that is more fun than fun can be.*

*Smiles abound for you and me, always talking and laughing
with the divine Trinity. But how you live your life you must decide,
goes according to God you must abide.
If you do enter the sacred tiny door,
and love will flow to those with forgiving hearts.
Real love and loyalty Our Father sees that friends will never be parted.
Now my duty is done to bring life to those with Esprit.*

*Embrace his sacred will says the good news servant me.
Sing God's songs of love. His children danced the ways of His melody.
So gently I freely give to those who want to hear, see, love into eternity.*

Your Life's Purpose in God's Grand Design

To know to experience God's real love and sacred morality.
Narrow is the path for the choice of the few,
close to their goal singing so merrily
bowing down to enter the gate of the Heavenly.
Keep close the sacred and divine, God will guide you to the Heavenly

34

What Happens When People Die?

My dearest Lord in Heaven, I am interested in what happens with people after they pass away and enter into the spiritual realm as mature human adults. In this book, my dear Lord and Savior, there is a picture of a person standing in front of a fork in the road. It is simple to see the decision in front of you. Do you lead a life of love, putting other people ahead of you and making their lives more joyous, or do you choose the other road of satanic sin, putting yourself ahead of everyone else? It truly is that simple. One road leads to eternal bliss in Heaven, and the other road leads to hell.

And how does this moment in time relate to the great judgment of all people within Christianity?

AFTER DEATH, EVERYONE ENTERS THE SPIRITUAL REALM

November 27, 2022
Jesus Christ

My dear son, people die they are indeed escorted into the spiritual realm. It is here that they are shown all the good and bad of their lives. I am there with them along with a number of angels. All of this is conducted in a very loving atmosphere. There is no finger-pointing, no blame, not the slightest hint of any anger, and they are put into a position where all around them is felt pure love.

They can feel the love of angels and me and they can see for themselves how they react to feeling love. When we show them all the details of their life and show them the occurrences of when they showed other people love and consideration versus when they exploited other people,

hurt them, plotted against them, murdered them, cheated, and all the other heinous crimes against Almighty God's sacred children.
A LIFE REVIEW IS CONDUCTED

October 14, 2022
Jesus Christ

It is within the atmosphere of love that they are shown their lives and unfortunately to most people the vast majority cannot bear to watch what they have done. It is horrifying to them to see themselves within an atmosphere of love doing the very things they remember doing. This brings them into the contrast of how a child of God with their free will should conduct themselves in their lives that has been given to them versus what they actually did with their lives and how they either promoted the well-being of others of God's children and loved them in so many different ways or how they helped destroy and cause great harm and grief to God's children.

It is at this point within an atmosphere of love that they have a chance to understand just how far they have with their free will wandered away from us within the Trinity and the laws their Almighty Father has laid down to govern their behavior on earth.

There comes a point during this examination of their life when they realize that they are very ill fit and unworthy to enter the gates of Heaven solely based on what they saw themselves do in their lives. They come to realize that by not entering the Heavenly realm they will be able to continue their behavior as they did when they were alive. They will be with people who to varying degrees of sinfulness will accept them as they are. In a real sense they will feel like they have more freedom now because they can do whatever they wish, they can continue to rob cheat steal or do any other evil actions and not be punished in the way that they would be when they were alive on earth. To these kinds of people that have mutilated their free will into seeking domination over the others in Satan's realm, this will seem like a great opportunity for them.

SOME ARE DESTINED FOR INESCAPABLE HELL

However, at some point they will realize that there is no gratification in anything they do. There is no fulfillment, there is no love there is no sense of accomplishment. Their existence becomes something that is worse than their most horrible nightmares. For then they realize that there is no improvement, there is no chance to escape their situation.

After a time further on they will begin to notice that they are slowly coming apart. This is because Almighty God has set into place the law of entropy. This is an ever-increasing amount of random chaos, separation and ultimately evaporation into nothingness. This is when the real terror of their inescapable fate will descend upon them. It will be with them as long as they are able to think and have a sense of self which will be destroyed by entropy at an increasing rate over the timeline they are on. This process will continue until there is absolutely nothing left, only nothingness.

The entropy that Jesus speaks of is the same physical force I have discussed several times throughout this Biblical material. Again, it is a measurement of the randomness or chaos within a closed system. That is the scientific definition. Within our physical universe, which is tied to the spiritual universe, the people that are confined to hell are confined to a closed system. There is no escape for them. Thus, over time entropy will continue to increase faster and faster as it currently is doing within the physical universe, which we call the cosmos, and our galaxy, which we call the Milky Way. It is happening right now, and we humans call it aging.

However, to people forever confined to hell, a very small part of the spiritual realm, they will fly apart faster and faster until their consciousness and self-awareness ultimately disintegrate into the complete nothingness from which they came. Unlike what our childhood Bible teacher said, there is no eternal fire and brimstone. There never was, and there never will be. Besides, what loving Father would ever do that to his sacred children? Nope, nobody.

Your Life's Purpose in God's Grand Design

35

What Happens When Unrepentant Sinners Die?

July 25, 2022, 01.12 PM

Dear Lord,
I have often wondered what happens to people who have sinned so much in their lives, mostly by putting themselves ahead of others of God's children. They do so through outright crimes and so many other ways. One way in particular that I hear often is that many people say things like, "I want to do it my way." Frank Sinatra, in his heyday, popularized the song with that title. He made millions of dollars. He was part of the rat pack and was an egotist.

I am not sure what that even means. What do they mean by "it "? This is even after it is explained to them that they need to accept the overwhelming love of Almighty God and accept his rules of life. What happens to these people when they arrive in your presence after they die?

Our Lord God Answers:

My dearest son I have been with you every moment of your entire life and I will be with you for all eternity for you have overcome the harshest of suffering both mentally and physically. It is because you have kept your faith in your Father in Heaven and us in the Trinity and also kept your promise before you were born when you said that you wanted to put other people before yourself, it is because of this that your Father in Heaven is allowing you to hear our words and publish them in this book.

You are the only one that has been gifted this way and also because in your life you have gained the knowledge, the wisdom, and the talent to write this book. You are the only one. We love you ever so very much my dearest son. You bring great delight to us and we look forward to spending eternity with you and your loved ones.

With this in mind my dear son I will now answer your question. When a person arrives before us after their death and after they have rejected their Father in Heaven and the rest of the Trinity, they are presented with their life history and set before them. It is then they realize the depth of their crimes and their wicked sinfulness. It is then they are asked for an explanation of why they behaved in such a heinous manner. It is shown to them all the times in their life that they could have chosen the Godly path and the path of love but they rejected it. It is only then that they beg for forgiveness. But as it is explained in the Bible, I say to them I never knew you, depart from me. Then an angel escorts them to the gates of hell from which they shall never escape.

Each person is shown their life history with all the decisions they made and all the actions they took and especially how they treated others of God's children. It is from these things that it is chosen what their destination will be.

For you my dear son this will be a joyous formality and it will be attended by so many angels and people from Heaven that love you so very much. And as I have said before to you, a portion of you is already here in Heaven. You have heard comments from people here in the Heavenly realm that can only come from your presence here. Continue with this excellent book and continue with your good work spreading your Father's and my gospel to all people you meet and come into contact with. For this is the purpose of your life and you have done very well. I love you.

Dear reader, all of the above is what our God in Heaven, the Trinity, told me that afternoon in July 2022. In some ways, I'm very embarrassed and humbled to include this in this book, yet on the other hand, it contains valuable information regarding what happens to people right after they die. What more can I add to this? Nothing. But there are other topics related to this that I also asked the Trinity that will be presented in other places within this book.

36

Spiritual Warfare

THE COSMIC SPIRITUAL WARFARE SITUATION

If you are a Christian today, you are involved in spiritual warfare even if you do not understand it or realize it for what it is. Spiritual warfare has been now intensifying for decades. Our Bible tells us that this would happen.

All of this started when Lucifer rebelled against our Almighty Father in Heaven. When Satan was cast down from Heaven to this earth, all negativity, emotional problems, and destruction came with him to our planet. It is true to say that all negativity, all problems, destruction, broken relationships, and crime have as their ultimate source with Satan and his demons, who occupy the spiritual realm while Satan is the prince of this earth.

Remember as covered earlier in this book, the spiritual realm does overlap with the physical realm. Our bodies have two general aspects. The spiritual and the physical. This matches precisely the two realms of physical and spiritual. "*Spiritual warfare is the cosmic conflict waged in the invisible, spiritual realm what is simultaneously acted out in the visible physical realm*."

Nothing happens in the physical realm unless it occurs first in the spiritual minds of men. All ideas originate first in the minds of men. It is the minds of human beings that can be considered Satan's playground. Satan uses many tricks upon us to lull us into sin. Remember what he did with Adam and Eve. This sin is then manifested into our physical world that we live in every day of our lives. Also, remember that the Angels of God operate in the spiritual realm. I can only imagine the kinds of conflict between the Angels of God and the demons of Satan within the spiritual realm.

SPIRITUAL WARFARE AND THE FALL OF AMERICAN CHRISTIAN VALUES AND PRINCIPLES

In Hebrews 1:14, "Are not all angels ministering spirits sent to serve those who will inherit salvation." I have been on this planet for 75 years. I grew up in the 1950s. I remember very well the solid and good value system and ethics and principles of behavior that existed in our society during those years. It was one of hard work to get what you want. Get off your butt and go to work. Treat everyone as you would want to be treated.

Although simple, these principles became our great country's backbone and birthright. The United States of America, through its Constitution and Bill of Rights, propelled our society to one of "*if you want something, you have to work for it*." And work all the people did so they may achieve a better life for themselves and their families. Over the ensuing decades, I have watched and observed in complete dismay how our country was eroded at its foundations, its values, and principles of existence.

I am surprised, however, at the enormous number of people in our country that have fallen away from Christian values and choose to manipulate our socialist government into them paying the legions of plainly lazy people living off the hard work and taxes of honest good people. Whether you realize it or not, we are in a grave spiritual war with Satan and his demons. The increasing influence of Satan into our culture over the years now threatens the very existence of our country, which is based on Godly principles of life, liberty, and the pursuit of happiness. Looking back, it becomes clear that this degeneration of Christian values and our constitutional responsibilities all started with the hippie movement in the 1960s. From there, with their values of "free love," "if it feels good, do it," and "rebel against the man," along with drugs served to initiate an increasingly popular value system that would go on to infect our society in many different forms.

Freedom requires, without excuse, responsibility by every citizen. The hippie counterculture worked to destroy individual responsibility. Strangely and ironically enough, it is because of the overwhelming success of implementing Godly values within our political, economic, cultural, and familial values that we have generated such great wealth for the health and well-being of our citizens.

Now because of the great economic system we have built on Godly principles, we have enough money for a corrupt and satanic government to tax away trillions of dollars from hard-working citizens and give it to Democrat-favored groups of people and organizations that will perpetuate their anti-God political power to continue their destruction of the very taxpayers that make it all possible.

Heinous liberals will soon turn to tyranny and a police state to continue extracting the hard-earned money that honest, hard-working taxpayers can provide under constant threats and duress.

As this is written, the Democrat Congress has now authorized hiring 87,000 more IRS agents armed with weapons and the government permission to shoot taxpayers. This is as of August 2022. It will not go well with Almighty God when people that support this are judged. Hell will overflow with new prisoners.

SPIRITUAL WARFARE AND SATAN'S AGENDA

"*Satan uses all manner of deceptions in order to accomplish his agenda of bringing the world under his influence and control.*"

First, Satan's target are individuals of God's children. In 1 Peter 5:8, "be of sober spirit, be alert. Your adversary, the devil, prowls around like a roaring lion, seeking someone to devour." In other words, Satan is after YOU! Back in the 1950s, when I grew up, there was a very popular saying, "idle minds and hands are the devil's playground."

Do not be fooled. This is completely true whether you realize it or not. Many times, Satan has surreptitiously encouraged the use of drugs, alcohol, relationships, sex, bitterness, hopelessness, discouragement, low self-esteem, depression, arrogance, and codependency. All this will come between the children of God and their Creator in Heaven.

Our Democrat president Biden and Congress have encouraged a completely open border to Mexico where millions of pounds of deadly drugs like fentanyl, heroin, and other deadly drugs manufactured in China and distributed by drug cartels in Mexico. The Democrat party purposely ignores all this, which causes the death of many thousands of American citizens. This is pure satanic behavior aimed at the destruction of the next two generations in the United States of America. Democrats purposely ignore all of this and have untold amounts of blood on their hands. Democrats are the party of Satan and his demons.

Secondly, Satan targets the family. We see this horror right before our very eyes in our society today. Since 1971 has murdered 64 million developing human beings while they were still in their mother's wombs. This is horrific beyond any dimension. The promoter of this in our Christian society is the Democratic Party. Their abortion slogan is "<u>my body, my choice</u>." They ignore the child of God that is developing within the mother's womb. Why? To get more votes for political power by perverted people with no morals in the Democratic Party.

Third, Satan targets our very own Christian churches. Over the years I have seen the erosion of pure Christian values in the Catholic Church. The sexual abuse of children by priests some time ago is a raging example of the <u>*evil that has penetrated the agreeable to evil minds of Christian priests and ministers*</u>. Another sign is there are pictures of <u>*Pope Francis wearing a homosexual rainbow medallion around his neck right beside the cross of Jesus.*</u> This is complete heresy in the most perverted sense possible. I can only imagine what this Pope does behind closed doors. Why don't the Cardinals get rid of this perversion? It is because of all the snakes, demons, and reptiles that exist within their own closet.

Fourth, Satan targets our entire society as a whole. <u>*In Daniel chapter 10, we see how Satan is behind the rulers of the nation.*</u> We all know about Hitler, Mussolini, Idi Amin, Kim Jong Un, and a long list of atrocities.

Note: *the above four targets of Satan are taken from the book written by Pastor Tony Evans,* **Victory In Spiritual Warfare**. *I strongly encourage everyone to read his book, for it is very insightful and filled with good information on how Christians can successfully battle Satan and his demons.*

The United States of America has been disintegrating away from God's laws, values, and principles for many decades now. It is all because of Satan in the minds of willing people who consciously, for their evil purposes, go along satanic principles and actions against their fellow Godly children.

The larger our federal and state governments became, the more and more our society and fundamental principles were eroded. In the 1950s, the federal government budget, the total budget was $100 billion. Now we speak in many hundreds of trillions of dollars taxed away from hard-working citizens on a "vote for me basis." There are so many government giveaway programs from working people to those described through political reasons as needy, downtrodden, discriminated against, and all other sorts of excuses so they would get free money out of the pockets of the working taxpayer of this country.

Politicians give enormous amounts of taxpayer money to special interest groups likely to vote for them. They use any excuse under the sun to do this. Democrats are actively supporting and aiding the communist regime in China through increasingly favorable economic ties to China, not the American people. Pres. Biden even went so far as to give China a huge portion of our oil emergency reserves. This belongs to us, the American citizen. This makes the satanic Biden administration an enemy of us, the American citizen.

So, my dear children of God, we are in a desperate spiritual war with the satanic forces that eat away every Christian value and principle handed down to us by Almighty God himself. In the following pages, I will reveal to you how Satan and his demons have continually attacked me because I am a devoted Christian, and I dare to write Christian spiritual books for people like you.

SPIRITUAL WARFARE, MY FIRST AND DIRECT PERSONAL ENCOUNTER WITH SATAN VERY SCARY!

If you doubt that Satan exists or minimize it in your mind, I have shocking news for you that happened to me, your author. I have documented these stories in two of my previous six spiritual books. The first is" My Real Life Christian Spiritual Journey," and the second is, "The Divine Resting On My Shoulder." But I will repeat here what has already been written.

This terrible attack by Satan himself occurred when I was married to my late wife Marilyn for only a few years, and we had one infant daughter. It was early in the morning before the sun rose, and we were sleeping in bed. The day before, I realized that I was indeed a Christian deep in my heart, and I got very angry with Satan for all the destruction he wreaks upon the world. So being in my mid-20s at that time and unfamiliar with the power and reality of the spiritual world and the constant warfare within that realm, I cursed Satan directly a number of times. I told him I hated him for what he was doing and that I wanted him to stop.

Unknown to me, my outburst against Satan and his satanic world got his attention. A few days later, as I said above, we were sleeping in the early morning hours. Then suddenly, without warning, I heard ever so loudly the words, "I will get you!" "I will get you!" "I will get you!" These words were so loud that I thought even the neighbors would hear them shouting at me. I turned over and put my head up to see a horrifically ugly form of blackness, pure blackness shouting these words at me. All this only took perhaps 15 or 20 seconds.

ACTIONS

I rolled over, nudged my wife, and said, "did you hear that?" She responded by saying, "here what?" Somehow the horrific loud hateful, dripping, and drenched with such hate that I had never experienced before was not heard by anyone else but me. I thought that was impossible, but even my wife lying next to me, did not hear anything. This was so confusing to me.

I cannot begin to describe the terror and fear that the appearance of a deeply black figure would appear at the foot of my bed and yell those words above, "I will get you!" To say that I was frightened out of my wits would be an understatement for words cannot contain the absolute horror of what I had just experienced. Needless to say, I could not sleep any more that night. I don't remember telling my wife anymore about what had just happened. Then, our infant daughter woke up shortly afterward, and we started to attend to her needs.

This horrific experience suddenly brought me to the reality of Satan's existence and the spiritual realm, which I had only heard about in mass at church and in the first four years at St. Tarcissus elementary school in Chicago. This experience was like a gigantic, huge hammer coming down on me, and I was scared to death. My detailed memories of this awful experience have never left me.

Since then, over the years, I could see that Satan was continually attacking me in my mind by somehow shoving completely unwanted and very negative thoughts at me. They just seemed to come out of nowhere. Over time I grew spiritually to discern the difference between my thoughts, divine thoughts, and knowing when it comes from the satanic realm. I knew when it was Satan, but I did not know how to fight back. This realization and the accumulated knowledge that I now have propelled me to include this section about spiritual warfare in this book. I will need to reveal the personal battle I fight against Satan daily.

HOW TO DEFEAT SATAN IN A WORLD OF SPIRITUAL WARFARE.

As for me, when I wake up in the morning, I swing my legs over the side of the bed. I stretch somewhat and then say the Our Father and the Hail Mary. Then I ask God the following question, "Dear Lord, who am I? This sounds very strange and is not intended for you. I must do this because I am a big target for Satan and his demons. Many times, Satan attempts to pose as our Lord and Savior Jesus Christ and our blessed Mother Mary to trick me into believing what he says is coming from God. So, I ask our Father to tell me who I am because only our Father in Heaven can address me as "His Child" or "His Son." I am like you, a child of God.

There have been many times when Satan tried to pose as God. But Satan or any of his demons can never call me "My Child." So, to check to confirm who I am talking to, I ask, "who am I"? If the answer comes back that I am "His Child" or my son, then I know for sure that I am talking to God. If, on the other hand, the answer comes back that I am "Richard." Then I know it is Satan or a demon. If that is the case, I tell them forcefully, "In the name of my Lord and Savior Jesus Christ, I command you to go back to hell where you belong. Go NOW!" Satan must comply, or he will be severely punished, which he has done quite a number of times.

I have lived my life as a prime target for Satan. He knew before what I was, a devoted Christian who loves Almighty God and our Savior and Lord Jesus Christ along with, of course, the Holy Spirit which precedes from them. His attacks against me increased greatly as I started writing the first of my six Christian spiritual books.

After praying a lot to God, asking Him to remove Satan's attacks from me in the morning and throughout the day, I have come to enjoy a life where any attacks from Satan are now far fewer and farther in between. The lesson here for you is that God does answer our prayers. You will not let any of his children lose spiritual warfare to Satan. The only way is if his children purposely and willfully allow that to happen.

THE BEST WAYS FOR CHRISTIANS TO WIN THE SPIRITUAL WAR

My dear Christians fighting the spiritual war can be very tiring, but this is where you should never give up. The following are different ways to fight and win against Satanic effects in your life.

First, you should start each day with prayer as you get out of bed. Say an Our Father, a Hail Mary, and any other of your favorite prayers. Greet Almighty God by saying something like "good morning, Father, good morning, my Lord and Savior Jesus" and "good morning, my dear Blessed Mother Mary.

Second, throughout the day, talk to God. You do not have to say anything out loud. All of this is spoken within your mind telepathically, which is the portal to the spiritual world and the Heavenly realm. Even though you may feel it's like a one-way conversation, it is not, for your Heavenly Father loves to communicate with you. He hears every word you say to Him. In return when you speak with your Father in Heaven you may get a feeling, an idea, or some kind of response. Look for that. Ask your Father in Heaven to respond to you immediately with his voice. If you do not ask your Father, then He will not speak. So, ask Him to speak to you. You will be surprised by the number of times you will indeed hear his voice one way or another. But also remember that your Father has many different ways that He can speak to you in response to anything you ask Him or tell Him. But again, ask your Father to respond to you immediately, for you are listening for Him.

You may also ask Him to give you a clear sign, like perhaps a spiritual vision of our Lord and Savior Jesus Christ and our blessed Mother Mary. Don't be surprised if this request is indeed granted to you. All of this suggested prayer and conversation with Almighty God is never wasted. At the end of the day, when it is time to sleep, always end your day with prayers. You can easily repeat your morning prayers and then say good night to your Father in Heaven, the Holy Spirit, our Lord and Savior Jesus Christ, and our blessed Mother Mary. And thank them for the preceding day and any other thoughts and requests you may have.

Lastly, I suggest you read this book written by Pastor Tony Evans. There are other good books as well, but I find this one very useful: Victory In Spiritual Warfare. Harvest House Publishers

Victory In Spiritual Warfare, Pastor Tony Evans, Harvest House Publishers, 2011

37

What Happens When We Pray?

I prayed for my dear wife Evangeline's knee to be healed. I asked God this question. What happens when we pray? If we pray for healing, how does that take place? If we want to affect an event, how can that be guided to a good result by prayer? What are the factors involved and the mechanisms in play?

Our Heavenly Father answered me directly, as He always does in plain English. The below text is precisely what He told me without any changes from me. I did not interpret anything. As He spoke, this is what He revealed to me in my thoughts.

ALMIGHTY GOD HEARS EVERY PRAYER

June 6, 2022, 10:47 AM
Our Heavenly Father

When you pray to me, Almighty God, first of all I hear every prayer that you say no matter what it is. This is true for everyone. I consider the circumstances that exist around the situation. If it is according to my will, I will grant what is being prayed for. In the case of Evangeline's knee, I will use natural healing process and amplify it so her knee will heal and heal faster.

When you prayed so much for Marilyn's healing from cancer, it was not my will that she be completely healed. Rather because of what you did for her, my son, I extended her life far beyond what it would have been had you not prayed for her and as a Reiki master given her prayerful Reiki treatments. This is why she lived an additional five years instead of the normal 18 months given her situation. Your Father in Heaven has the ability to focus His healing power on Evangeline's knee in this case.

I know you understand scientific matters so I will explain it further this way. In matters of healing something has gone wrong for whatever reason within a person's body. The body has natural healing ability but sometimes it gets overwhelmed due to accident, disease, and other things. The physical law of entropy says all things will decay and the order of bodily functions becomes more chaotic, and some intervention is required for healing. Your Father in Heaven granted your prayer to Him to heal Evangeline's knee. He set in motion amplified healing processes so that she will get better relatively soon. It is not instantaneous like many people believe. God created all healing processes for the human body and in cases of healing He simply amplifies those to the extent necessary to heal whatever is wrong.

Outside of the human body there are many actions that take place that people pray to me to affect a different outcome. All exterior events are always initiated by human minds. This is except those events such as natural disasters. As you know my dear son, God dwells within each of you. He uses his power to nudge people's minds in such a way as to affect their future actions either avoid a bad circumstance or to take action that will result in the good outcome for everybody.

In this latter case, all too many people are just not listening to their inner self where God dwells. So, praying to your Father may not do any good which is precisely what Satan wants. He wants the minds of people to be blinded so they cannot hear what the small inner voice of your Father wants to tell them. Some people call it conscience, but it goes far deeper than that. Your minds are connected to the spiritual realm, and this is where Satan plays his sinful games. And so, he plants sinful seeds and desires contrary to the will of your Heavenly Father.

Some people have damaged emotions within their minds. This is almost always the result of trauma. Your Father in Heaven can certainly help in these situations as He is so very close to his suffering child. Praying for a person in that situation can yield healing but it always takes time through the natural processes of the human mind. Your prayers will indeed speed up the healing process. But some people have a blocked mind regarding Almighty God. Depending on the strength of this blockage, it can either slow down the healing process or even prevent it entirely. (Is all of this clear to you my dear son?)

Then I said yes, my Lord, it is clear to me now that I asked. Thank you so much for increasing my understanding regarding this part of our existence. I love you, dear Lord.

IT WILL BE GRANTED IF IT'S ACCORDING TO HIS WILL

Hebrews 13:6 — The New King James Version (NKJV)
⁶ So we may boldly say: *"The Lord is my helper, I will not fear. What can man do to me?"*

38

The Lords Prayer

The **Our Father** has been with us ever since Jesus Christ walked the face of the earth. This prayer is recited by Christians throughout the world millions of times each day. When the Lord's disciples asked Him how to pray, He responded by saying the fundamental words of the Our Father. Let's break this down in some detail based on the wonderful words of the Our Father.

"Our Father who art in Heaven" [14] [15]
These few words establish our intimacy with our Father in Heaven, He is Abba (our Daddy). God is ever so close to us because He is our Father. Not only that but these words bring to mind a parental relationship, the Creator of all his sacred children. It also brings to mind his authority and power over us with his guidance and love for us his sacred children on this earth. Additionally, when we become Christian and accept God into our lives, we also become his heirs in Heaven. This means that we will enjoy with God all his deep abundant joy and fulfillment in Heaven which is incorruptible for all eternity. There is so much meaning is so few but ever so important words.

"Hallowed be thy name"
What we are praying here is that we want to make the name of God Holy. It means that God should be set apart and be the highest of all. When we hallow the name of God above all, peace will break out among us in our own heart. When we hallow God above all, then we become rightly ordered and just and live our lives accordingly.

---

[14] Matthew Chapter 6
[15] Inspired by Bishop Robert Baron, "On The Our Father", YouTube

"Thy Kingdom come, thy will be done, on earth as it is in Heaven"
This does not mean his Kingdom is established on earth. No, it is ridden with sin here which is vile in nature. Rather it means that the right order among the Angels and the saints in Heaven is their order of love as the foundation of the Kingdom. The order of nonviolence, selfless love be one with the voices of the Angels as they sing their praises of God, that we may be harmonized among ourselves as the Angels are in Heaven. Let thy will be done on this earth as it is already done in Heaven.

"Give us this day our daily bread"
There is a translation situation here in the Bible from the Greek. The word daily only appears once in the Greek, and all other places another word means "super substantial". This is very important. The correct translation should be "give us this day our super substantial bread".

As Catholics we refer to this bread as the substantiated bread whose substance has been transfigured into the substance of the body of Jesus Christ. So, this is actually a prayer for the mass. It is a prayer for communion with Jesus Christ. Not the daily subsistence bread for living from day to day. This is a strong reference to communion with God even though the English translation does not indicate that.

"And forgive us our trespasses as we forgive those who trespass against us"
One of the main themes of the teachings of our Lord Jesus Christ is that of forgiveness. Within mankind or the children of God we have great difficulty in forgiving people that have hurt us. But it is taught by our Lord Jesus Christ that this is mainstream and is a manifestation of love for your fellow man. Even large groups of ethnic people carry grievances for a very long time within their hearts against other peoples on the earth. I remember my very religious grandma. She always would say that "we should never trust a Serbian". This common hatred between the two groups is carried on for hundreds of years and even into the mind of my very pious Catholic grandma.

"And lead us not into temptation but deliver us from evil."
Early on in the Old Testament it can be shown that all the happenings within life are the result of the actions of Yahweh. If something bad happens within the family or to someone personally, it is because

somewhere somehow, they have sinned and now they are being punished for what they did by Almighty God.

"For thine is the Kingdom and the power and the glory now and forever, Amen"
This in many ways is reasserting the first line in this prayer. Jesus also said to the disciples that you may pray many different ways. This I have given you is not the only way. But you will be well served to use this as a model for your prayers in the future.

39

Our Prayer Hail Mary

Like most Christians, my favorite prayers are the Our Father and the Hail Mary. These are wonderful prayers that recognize the fundamental theology of Christianity. You may have other prayers also that are your favorites; all I can say about that is, "God bless you for that." As I did with the Our Father, now I will address the prayer to our Holy Blessed Mother Mary. This is a short prayer loaded with wonderful love for all of us Christians.

Hail Mary full of grace,
I cannot comment on this phrase better than what is on the Bible study website. This is part of what they say about Mary being full of grace. "How does the Bible define the word "grace?" Is it merely the fact that God likes us? It is an important concept as the King James Bible records the word 170 times. They know it came through Jesus Christ (John 1:14, 17).

When Paul wrote the words ". . . for you are not under law but under grace" (Romans 6:14), He used the Greek word charism (Strong's Concordance #G5485). God saves us by this charism. Since this is the mode of a Christian's salvation, it is of paramount importance and something the devil is trying his best to hide and confuse its true meaning! The scriptures say Jesus grew in charism (Luke 2:52), which is translated as "favor" in the KJV. If charism means unmerited pardon in Luke 2...."

The Lord is with thee, Blessed art thou amongst women,
Luke 1:28 And having come in, the angel said to her, "Rejoice, highly favored one, the Lord is with you; blessed are you among women!"

This is from the Gospel of Luke, exactly the source of the next phrase in our prayer Hail Mary. The angel said Mary was highly favored. In this word, favored is a synonym for the word grace. We could call this wonderful prayer "Hail Mary Highly Favored." But remember, the word grace is used a hundred and 170 times in the King James version of our sacred Bible. For this reason, it is most appropriate to use the word grace and not favored.

And blessed is the fruit of thy womb, Jesus
This phrase is so very beautiful and simple. Frankly, it is self-explanatory. The word blessed or blessing is used to invoke God's power and care upon a person, on a place or on a thing, or on an endeavor of some kind. A blessing is very powerful and invokes God's power to be with all of the above.

Holy Mary Mother of God,
This phrase is also simple but very beautiful and deep in its meaning. The phrase "Mother of God" has extremely important and deep meanings for Christianity. All Christians have said this prayer many times in their life without realizing the depth and importance of this three-word phrase.

This phrase is central to Almighty God's plan for all his children's redemption. Mary was a human being on earth. Through her obedience to Almighty God, she bore a child that was both fully human and fully divine. Her child Jesus was indeed fully part of the Trinity and fully part of earthly children. It is Mary that enabled the establishment of this link along with her son Jesus soon to be called Jesus Christ. Together they formed the necessary linkage and relationship between Heavenly and physical earthly realms. Without Mary and her son Jesus God's plan for redemption would not exist.

Whether Christians understand this or not, this phrase is pivotal to God's plan for redeeming his children from their sinful state of being. Through her child Jesus Christ, we can all be redeemed and join God in the Heavenly realm and enjoy paradise with God and the Trinity for all eternity. I hope I have made this clear enough for you to understand the monumental importance of this very simple yet enormously pivotal in history making the phrase, Mother of God.

Pray for us sinners now and at the hour of our death, Amen
This obviously is a prayer to Mother Mary to pray for us sinners to our Father in Heaven. Our Blessed Mother Mary's prayers are very powerful because of her Heavenly position. Most people do not remember the role that Mary will play in the final defeat of Satan and his demons. It is so written that it is Mary that will crush the head of Satan. This is strong language to indicate that it is the Mother of God and the Mother in many ways of all of us that will play a direct role in the eternal defeat of Satan once and for all.

As we all should know, it is our Mother that will defend us under all circumstances. And so be it that the Mother of God is in many ways the Mother of us all. She will protect her children. And she will continually pray for all of us to our Father in Heaven to protect us from all the dangers we face in this Satan-filled world that we currently live in. But take heart, as we are only visiting this world before we return to our eternal home with her Father in Heaven.

Bible Study: https://www.biblestudy.org/beginner/what-is-grace.html

40

A True Story of A Little Boy, Child of God

Our story begins when this little boy was still in the heavenly kingdom. There is one such sacred child, who was different from all the others as each of God's children are. It was decided that his theme for his earthly life would be to always put the needs of others ahead of himself. This theme basically emulates the characteristics of our Father in Heaven. This greatly pleased his father. This was a monumental decision by this little boy. It would determine the path of his existence as a physical human being while on earth. It also made him a prime target for Satan. It is because this little boy reflected a fundamental characteristic of Almighty God.

As Satan hated Almighty God so very much, his hatred for this little boy now made him a prime target for Satan to destroy. During this time in the heavenly Kingdom and before it was his turn to be born on earth, he developed spiritually into a very sensitive and perceiving child. He loved to watch how things interacted together and observed how things worked. He was very inquisitive. He also said something very special to his Father while he was in heaven. He knew at some time it would be his turn to be born on earth. So, he told his Father that most of all he wanted to live a life where he would put the need of others ahead of himself. Satan was waiting for him the moment he was born and began his program of destruction.

When the boy was born into the world, it turns out that he became an only child to his parents that did not want him at all. His father was quoted as saying when seeing the little infant, "I did that!?" They argued a lot about our little boy's intended arrival on earth to them as his parents. Even before this little boy was born, he was already perceived as a big problem. His earthly father was a very cruel and cold man. He gave our little boy many and frequent beatings and punishments and constant threats of punishments and he yelled at the little boy very often. His father denied him much of the pleasures of being a child. His mother did nothing to stop his father from his cruelty. It was not only many different kinds of undeserved punishments, but it was also the denial of any real expression of love for him. They showed all of creation that they did not love him or wanted him. His mother never once said "I love you". She never carried the little boy nor feed him while holding him as an infant, always putting him back on the bed.

Neither of his parents ever said "I love you" to the little boy. He was treated like he was a temporary visitor in his own home. Late in the little boy's life he found out that neither of his parents ever wanted him to be born. He was an only child and an outcast from his parents. Loneliness, PTSD, and depression followed this little boy through his childhood and throughout all his adulthood. His traumatic childhood also had the physical effects of being thin and frail along with chronic breathing problems and severe headaches for his entire life to this very day.

This is the legacy of what parents can do to their children. Growing up, all the little boy wanted was someone to love him. But the effects of the lack of love and cruelty toward him was profound. He became very afraid of other people especially authority figures, so he had very few friends. There is no doubt that it was Satan who had the greatest influence on both his parents. It is true that the closer you are to Almighty God, the harder it will be on earth because of Satan's pure hatred of God.

Yet his Holy father, the Holy Spirit and his Lord and Savior Jesus Christ were always so intimately close to him. Yet this little scared sacred boy could not feel that. This little boy felt completely alone in this world. He was completely scared of other people especially authority figures.

Throughout School
So, he turned to books and learning. He like chemistry and liked Mr. Healey his high school chemistry teacher. Later he figured out that to get away from the riff-raff students he needed to get very good grades and get on the tennis team. So, he did. Then he went to Santa Clara University as a Chemistry Major. This is when our little boy did not know it. But God was guiding him and protecting him from further hurt and pain. It

was then he met a Jesuit brother named Brother Bracco who became his life long friend to this day.

Early on then he met a wonderful woman and they were married for 38 years until his wife passed away leaving him three children that loved him. There is no doubt that it was God that arranged this for the little boy's happiness. It was years later that God again provided a most wonderful Christian woman that loves him so very much and they are still happily married to this day. She was a professor of theology. They will go to heaven together. God did indeed arrange his marriage to such a magnificent and loving woman. Even friends and relatives observed that, to them their marriage looked like it was indeed made in heaven.

It was! As the little boy grew older God revealed to him that there was not one second in his life that God was not with him every moment of every day. Because this little boy decided to put other people ahead of himself before he was born to this earth. When this little sacred child of God developed a fatal cancer, a very good doctor and a miracle from God that saved him from an early death. Even the doctor told him that "<u>you had invisible help in your healing</u> ". The doctor clearly indicated that <u>without some kind of miracle, medical treatment would not have saved him from an early death. Because of this miracle by Almighty God, you would not be reading this book,</u> the seventh spiritual book written by this little boy.

Starting when this little boy was about 50 years old he studied and obtained a master's degree in pastoral ministry with a minor in theology. That led to writing six books in Christian Spirituality. After that God approached this little boy with the most thrilling event of his life. Our Lord and Savior Jesus Christ, and our Blessed Mother Mary approached this now fully grown little boy to write this book that you are holding in your hands.

41

The Creation of This Book

For reasons not totally understood by this little boy now a full grown adult, Almighty God put his arms around this little boy and protected him until his time is finished on this earth. Blessed Mother also came to this little boy to nurture and protect him also. This little boy then could strongly see God's only begotten Son and our Blessed Mother standing next to him next to his right shoulder. Such great comfort this gave our little boy. God then gifted him with an intimate special relationship with Him such that our Lord in heaven could reveal to him so many details of God's creation both seen and unseen.

Both our Lord and Savior Jesus Christ and our Blessed Mother Mary approached this scared little boy who is me your author Rich Ferguson to help me write this magnificent book for your Christian spiritual knowledge. Nothing has been written like this since the Bible 2,000 years ago.

The little boy asked his Father why he was chosen for such a great honor to have many of the secrets of creation. The Trinity responded to him by saying, **"it is because of a decision you made to put other people ahead of yourself"**. *The little boy responded, "I do not remember making a decision like that". God responded,* **"you would not remember this my son, it is because you made this decision before you were born."** *Our little boy was completely astonished and happy. God also told this little boy that he was the first sacred child to have to have His permission about receiving detailed information of such secrets as what it was like before creation and the reasons for creation and how all of it is connected together.* Almighty God then told out little boy the following, **"regarding your book, I am well pleased"**. **"Do not cast your book to those who hate me"**.

Then God revealed to this special child so many things about the spiritual realm, heaven and how the physical universe was created and how they all relate to each other. This was revealed to our little boy during the time *he was writing this book that you are reading right now!* It is this special information revealed to our sacred little boy that you are reading within this book. God told this little boy that it is only him that he has given permission to understand much of the reality of God's creation and permission to publish it to all other of God's sacred children to read and learn from. Lastly, you may ask us any questions you will. We will answer you.

God also outlined to this child the details of his plan of redemption for all his children and why he created all that is seen and unseen. *The reason for creation is simply to provide his sacred children a direct pathway back to their father in heaven so they may spend the rest of eternity in a magnificent paradise where there are no limitations.* This became necessary because of the rebellion of Lucifer eons ago according to creation's timeline. All his children have to do is to accept and love their Almighty father in heaven and live their lives according to their fathers' commandments. It is this that will bring each of God's sacred children both fulfillment on earth and eternal life with our Father in Heaven for all eternity. There will be no end.

A second time to emphasize, This little boy in the last parts of his life became a Christian Minister and spiritual book writer. In this way and to this day he still puts other people and their needs above his own. In conclusion, very recently our loving Almighty God revealed to this grown-up little boy these words," *regarding your book, I am very well pleased.*"

It is now that you are reading the book written by this grown up little boy that very well pleased your Loving Almighty Father in heaven

42

This Is The End Of Our Magnificent Beginning Of Our Endless Lives

And so, it is almost all of us who have come to this earth to find out just how much we love our Father in Heaven through our birth.

Such courage it took for all of us immature children to come here after living with God for uncountable eons time, to know Him is to love Him from the bottom of our hearts. For Satan did not exist yet as us little children which we would be again before we were born unto this earth and naïve, so much fun as our Father we beheld as we ran around the cosmos giggling and laughing bouncing around playing tag and games as children do. We tried to play hide and seek but try to do that with your Father being already everywhere, couldn't be done! He was automatically cheating!

We laughed about that too! On and on our lives got better and better. As we played, we learned so much. We learned to play inter-dimensions as well when we started to know how to hide and seek and then we learned all about hiding in dimensions, Oh much fun that was. Then our Father was teaching us more and more about ourselves and our responsibilities and morality. Soon we realized that our playtime is coming to an end for Father was telling us that soon we would be born into another dimension and be taking on more responsibilities. So, we said yes. Because we knew something else was happening within creation something we did not like but it was affecting us in ways we did not know but we loved our Father so much and we wanted to help in ways we could. And our brother Jesus would tell us everything we needed to know. So, my dear brothers and sisters our lives will continue for all eternity our lives will constantly change and for us it will always change for the better because we love God and the Trinity loves us more and more as the eons pass us by. All of us love you so very much that will always increase and increase and increase again.

There is no end to our story.

God Loves You and God Loves Me Too

For Those In The Kingdom, Time Is Endless Joy

Read this book cover to cover in good health and I want to shake hands with you in the Heavenly Kingdom
Rich Ferguson

Your Life's Purpose in God's Grand Design

References and Footnotes

The Holy Bible, King James Version
The Holy Bible, New King James Version
A Brief History Of Time: Stephen Hawking
The Grand Design: Stephen Hawking
Hearing God: Peter Lord
Strong's Concordance
The Creator And The Cosmos: Hugh Ross
The Improbable Planet: Hugh Ross
A Real Life Christian Spiritual Journey: Richard Ferguson
The Divine Resting On My Shoulder: Richard Ferguson
Christians Alert, Democrats Are Attacking Our Country!: Richard Ferguson
The Origin Of Species: Charles Darwin
The Prophetic Voice Of God: Lana Vawser
Victory In Spiritual Warfare: Pastor Tony Evans
The Passion Of The Christ: Movie By Mel Gibson
The Our Father: Bishop Robert Barron (Youtube)
Bible.org:

https://anatomy.app/blog/human-anatomy
https://www.biblestudy.org/beginner/what-is-grace
https://www.britannica.com/science/aqueous-humor
https://www.openbible.info/topics/satan_rebellion
https://www.sciencefocus.com/the-human-body/dna
https://www.secretsunlocked.org/science

Richard Ferguson is available for book interviews and personal appearances. For more information contact:

Richard Ferguson
info@advbooks.com

I

To purchase additional copies of this book, visit our bookstore at:
www.advbookstore.com

Orlando, Florida, USA
"we bring dreams to life"™
www.advbookstore.com

www.ingramcontent.com/pod-product-compliance
Lightning Source LLC
Chambersburg PA
CBHW070532170426
43200CB00011B/2400